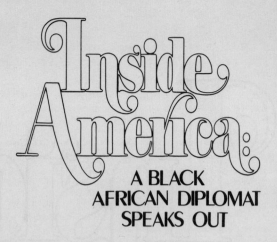

Inside America:

A BLACK AFRICAN DIPLOMAT SPEAKS OUT

 PUBLISHED BY **ACROPOLIS BOOKS LTD.**/WASHINGTON, D.C. 20009

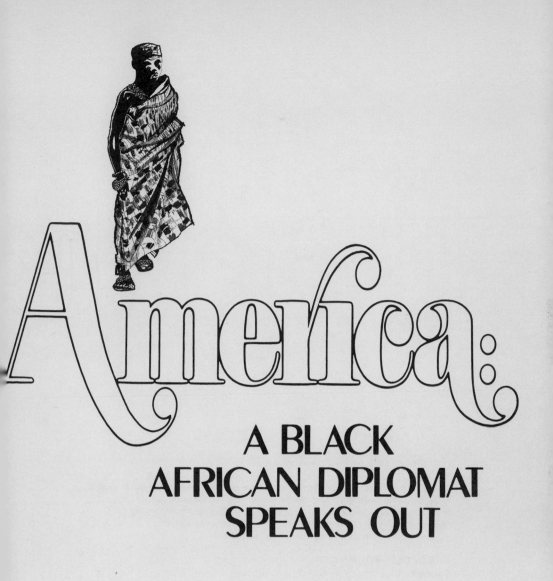

America:

A BLACK
AFRICAN DIPLOMAT
SPEAKS OUT

FRED KWESI HAYFORD

ACROPOLIS BOOKS LTD.
Colortone Building, 2400 17th St., N.W.
Washington, D.C. 20009

Printed in the United States of America by
COLORTONE PRESS Creative Graphics Inc., *Washington, D.C. 20009*

Type set in English
by Colortone Typographic Division, Inc.

Design by Design and Art Studio 2400, Inc.

Library of Congress Catalog Number 78-184716
Standard Book No. 87491-326-8

Acknowledgement

I wish to express my gratitude to the following persons who have directly or indirectly helped me to make this book possible.

(1) My favorite boss, H.E. Mr. E. M. Debrah, a man whose fantastic mind I have greatly benefited from. In spite of my respect and admiration for him, I never told him I was writing this book. I had intimated to him a couple of times that my intention, on returning home, was to leave the Diplomatic Service, and go into television. He advised against this, saying that he thought I had a future in the Diplomatic Service. I feared that if I confided in him he would dissuade me from writing since there is the likelihood that the Ghana Government might consider my book an embarrassment in its relations with the U.S.

(2) Hubert Bermont, the first person who was asked by my publisher to read the manuscript. He was brutally frank with me, but he also gave me plenty of encouragement.

(3) Dutton Ferguson, a Black accountant and freelance journalist who offered some useful advice.

(4) Joanne Blankespoor and Eileen Mason of Acropolis Books Ltd., who served as advisors and editors. Because of the nature of the book I was initially suspici-

ous of Mrs. Blankespoor's advice and suggestions. Eventually, I realized that she meant well, and that her advice, together with that of Mrs. Mason, has helped to make this book what it is.

Finally, I wish to express my thanks to A. J. Hackl, my publisher, for his sympathy, understanding and encouragement.

Fred Kwesi Hayford

Contents

"Thank You For Letting Me Be Myself"

I was born in a small, sleepy town called Elmina, located on the west coast of Ghana, the first African country south of the Sahara to have achieved political independence. Nothing much ever happens there. It is, however, a great tourist attraction. Sometimes I wonder whether the residents of any town in Ghana see as many foreigners carrying expensive camera equipment as the people of Elmina. The tourists come not only to see and take pictures of the magnificent bay that stretches six miles or more, but also to see one of Ghana's most famous historical landmarks, St. George's Castle. The Castle was built by the Portuguese in 1482 as a permanent trading post for themselves. The Portuguese were the first White men to have landed on Ghanaian soil. History shows that they obtained so much gold in the district between the rivers Ankobra and the Volta that they named the land "El Mina," the mine, and the French "Cote' de l'or," or

9

the Gold Coast, a name which the British later adopted for the entire country. In addition to the trade in gold the Portuguese also entered into the slave trade.

News of the profitable traffic in slaves and gold soon reached other nations, namely the Netherlands, England, France, Denmark, Sweden and Germany. By the eighteenth century the fierce competition for the slaves had begun.

As a child and later as an adult, I made several visits to St. George's Castle. I was shown its heavily fortified dungeons in which the slaves were kept; the markets where slave buyers came to bid; the windowless basement cells in which "unruly" slaves were imprisoned. Three quarters of these basement cells, according to historical literature, were filled with water as a means of punishing the slaves. I was shown the bat-infested narrow passageway in which the slaves, bound in chains, were led from their cells into waiting vessels.

All this had little effect on me. But when I was in my early twenties, I took two Black friends of mine who were working for the U.S. Embassy in Accra to Elmina. During a tour of the Castle, one of them broke down and wept like a child. For the first time in my life I realized that Black Americans had an association with the Castle that I did not have.

In Washington, a Black student from a high school in Baltimore, visiting the Embassy with his class, interrupted me during my commentary on a slide of the Castle. I had told the group I was from Elmina. "Mr. Hayford," the young man said, "If you are from Elmina, and this castle in the picture is where the slaves were kept and sold, then I can say that your great grandparents were responsible for what I and my people are going through today in America." "Right on," some of the students shouted, and "That's the truth," others joined in.

I am fairly sensitive, and was completely ruffled by the statement that the young man had made. Throughout the entire day, I tried to erase the incident from my memory but the more I tried the more I kept seeing visions of the young man making that statement. How could I have lived my life all these years without ever thinking that my own people were as guilty of the evils of slavery as the people who bought the slaves, and those who maltreated them? I realized that slavery was not only a case of demand and supply. It was also a case of supply and demand.

In the midst of apportioning blame, I suddenly remembered a long forgotten discussion that I once had with my grandmother on the whole question of slavery.

My father and I had been divided as to what I should do after my graduation from high school. I wanted to go into journalism. He was opposed to it. Journalists, he told me, only end up paying libel costs. He suggested law. For a whole year, I stayed home gainfully unemployed, while I tried to make a decision. To ease the boredom, I travelled to see some relatives that I had never met. During one of these visits, I fell in love with the daughter of an uncle of mine.

On my return to Elmina I told my mother and grandmother about the girl, and asked if they could arrange a marriage in the future. My mother dismissed the suggestion outright. She told me that living with my father in a city like Sekondi-Takoradi had ruined me. I had acquired so many sophisticated ideas and tastes that I would tend to expect too much from any girl I married. Since my uncle's daughter had not had the same background, chances were good that marriage would not work. My mother was absolutely right about my taste and ideas. In spite of advice from friends, I still expect too much from a woman. But what really surprised me about my mother was her ability to understand me so well even though we had never discussed such issues.

But it was my grandmother's objection to the girl that was a great eye-opener. She explained that even though my uncle, his brothers and sisters, and their children were close members of our extended family, none of them was a blood relation. My uncle's grandmother, my own grandmother explained to me, was a slave. That family had incurred a huge debt. Since the family had no visible means of repaying the debt from its own resources, they looked for someone who could settle the debt and accept in return the services of my uncle's grandmother.

I listened in disbelief as my grandmother told me the story, adding that it was a common practice in those days for very poor families to exchange their children for money. Once a slave was so purchased he could not go back to his own family. He or she was committed to loyal and devoted service to the family which bought him until he or she died. The slave was treated well or treated badly, depending on how the family was disposed towards him. Rich, childless women adopted the female slaves as their own children and at the owner's death, the slave received a sizeable amount of her property. Other slave owners treated the slaves well, but still drew a line of distinction between their own children and the slaves. Still other owners treated them poorly.

What my grandmother was telling me, in effect, was that although these descendants of the "slave" were now a part of my extended family, there were still people in Elmina who knew of this history. She feared that in a community like ours where people like to make references to a family's background during quarrels, someone might use the fact that I had been married to a descendant of a slave against me.

Until this revelation I did not have the slightest idea that internal slavery had actually existed before the arrival of the Portuguese on our soil. All this was unrecorded history, so when I reached school age, my teachers taught that tribal jealousies and warfare had been rampant before and at the time of the slave trade. Prisoners caught from these wars were sold to White men. The Portuguese, in other words, were making an existing market profitable.

Elmina has seen none of the little industrial development which has swept through Ghana since the date of independence. There are no jobs available for the people. As a result, young people leave Elmina for the larger cities in search of jobs immediately after graduation. The lack of job opportunities in Elmina has become the subject of teasing by our more fortunate neighbors. To this, the Elminians proudly reply, "We may have nothing, but don't you forget that no matter how worn out Elmina is, it was woven by the White man himself!" a proud reference to their early association with the first White men.

The pleasant monotony of life in Elmina is broken twice each year by two traditional festivals in which many of the people who have left the town return to visit. The festivals also attract other Ghanaians. The Elminians themselves come for many different reasons. Unmarried men, for instance, may come to meet for the first time the girls whom their parents are arranging for them to marry. Those who think that marriage through the arrangement of parents is a thing of the past may come to look around and see who is available. Some come for family reunions. Others come to ask for special favors from the family gods.

The first of these two festivals is celebrated on the first Thursday of January. Elminians still insist, in spite of 103 years of British colonial rule, that the first day of the new year is the first Thursday in January. No other day. On this day the ancestral spirits are remembered. Ghosts of dead friends and relatives are honored. If anyone needs a favor from the ancestral spirits and gods, this is the day that libations are poured and the requests are made.

The second festival, known as the River Festival, is held the first Tuesday of July. Traditionally, no fishing is allowed in any of Ghana's territorial waters on Tuesdays. It is generally believed that Tuesdays are the only days on which the gods that inhabit the sea, the rivers and the lakes take their rest. They should not be disturbed on those days. In Elmina, we pay homage to Benya, the river god, on the first Tuesday of July. In the homage, the other ninety-eight gods of Elmina are also remembered.

It is the belief of my people that the many gods are a part of creation. They are, in essence, the messengers of the Creator "Onyankopon" (God). Since human beings cannot directly communicate with the Supreme Being Himself, all of our requests to Him should be channeled through the lesser gods.

This explains the Ghanaian proverb "If you have a message for God you send it through the air." The lesser gods, represented by wooden structures, trees and other symbols, are each assigned a different duty—attending to the sun, sea, rain, harvest, etc. In some cases, certain ones provide guidance, health and prosperity to members of a clan or extended family.

Their abodes are considered sacred. Shrines are sometimes built in neighborhoods in which they dwell. Human functions such as sex, on these grounds, are forbidden. They would desecrate the area and incur the displeasure of the gods. To this day, if a girl in Elmina is ill and does not respond to treatment from either the hospital or the herbalist, her parents question her exhaustively for a confession that she has had relations with a man in a sacred place. If such a confession is obtained, a fetish priest is summoned to make a sacrifice.

For that reason, parents warn their daughters against any intimacy outside their homes. However, now that Christianity is firmly rooted in all of Ghana and three-quarters of our beliefs and traditions have been described as paganistic and primitive, many of the younger people do not care where such relations are performed.

It was at one of these festivals held to honor the god of the Benya River that my parents met. My father, as far as my tribe is concerned, was a stranger in Elmina. He was from another town, but had accompanied a friend of his to Elmina for the festival.

I have never asked him what were his reasons for going to the River Festival. But there he met my mother. They fell in love, and a year later I was born out of wedlock. He and my mother never received the parental consent and blessing that is so vitally important to a Ghanaian's marriage.

After I was born, I became a bone of contention. My father wanted the right to keep me. My grandparents on my mother's side disagreed. Finally, my father won the fight by using a threat most common among many Ghanaian men: "If you keep my child you will be responsible for his financial support. And should any harm come to him, I will hold you answerable."

This is a threat that no Ghanaian woman wants to hear. To an American, it has no great significance. But to

16

a Ghanaian woman, it is a heavy responsibility that she does not want to bring upon herself.

A great many divorced women are reunited with their husbands simply because a child becomes very sick. The assumption is that if the child is sick and does not get well in spite of treatment, his soul needs his father's care, and it is only that fatherly care which can restore his health. In a society where children are considered the most valuable asset, the mothers feel they have no alternative but to rush back to estranged or divorced husbands with ailing children.

My mother did not want any of these problems. So at the age of seven, I was moved from Elmina to Sekondi-Takoradi, Ghana's third largest city.

I loved my mother. Elmina had been my life, so it took me quite a while to become properly adjusted to Sekondi-Takoradi.

The people in Elmina were simple and down-to-earth. Everyone knew everyone else. One's frustrations and ill-luck were shared by all. One's good tidings were celebrated by all.

If I or any other child misbehaved publicly, any elderly person who saw me could discipline me. If he did not, he would report me to my mother, and my mother would be reprimanded for not exercising her proper function—the cane.

If someone died people did not shrug their shoulders and say "I don't know him, so I won't go to the funeral." Even if you did not know the dead man or woman, you knew someone who was related to him. It was a warm, close, caring place, and it broke my heart to leave Elmina.

My father, a strict disciplinarian, tried as much as he could to keep me away from Elmina. His views were very Ghanaian—that the father is the one who has the responsibility to train a child. But I missed Elmina so much that during my vacations I made up excuses that made him decide to send me back to visit. He may have done this reluctantly, but as the Ghanaians say: "It is only the stage of adulthood that not all of us have reached, but children we all have been." He understood my need for my mother.

The atmosphere in Sekondi-Takoradi was no less different from the one that I had been accustomed to in Elmina. If anything, Sekondi was bigger. More people lived there. The rents were higher and food a little more expensive. I missed the little backyard farm behind our house in Elmina into which one could walk any time of the day and pick a paw-paw, guava or pineapple, or even vegetables for cooking. Many of the people in Sekondi were buying chickens from markets when back in Elmina practically everyone I knew had their own little place where they reared chickens.

But Sekondi was, in a way, an eye-opener. By virtue of the fact that a great many of the people there had education and jobs, their patterns of living were slightly more sophisticated than those of the people in Elmina. At first it seemed frivolous to me that people were always discussing the dances that they had been to or the ones that they would go to. Back in Elmina dances are organized only when the festivals were held. In Sekondi dances were commonplace.

I also felt that the people dwelt too much on mannerisms and speech. Everything that one did was criticized as not conforming to the rules of etiquette. I was used to dipping my bread in coffee, tea and other beverages. In Sekondi I was told it was improper.

It was usual in Elmina to see families of four or five sitting together and eating from the same bowl. Only husbands or fathers were accorded the honor of eating from their own bowl. Some, however, ate either with their wives or the youngest of the children, the favorite. In Sekondi, I and my brother and sisters each had his or her own bowl or plate. It was unhealthy, I was told, for people to eat simultaneously from the same plate.

Only an insignificant number of the educated and the school-going crowd there were able to express themselves in the native tongue without loading their sentences with English words and phrases. "I am going to visit my uncle in Accra this weekend" for instance became "Moroko Accra weekend yi ake visit m'uncle." Some did it unconsciously. Others did it to impress. It was fashionable to integrate the native Fanti with English.

The situation was worse in my own middle class surroundings. My father was in the timber business, a very lucrative concern in those days. He had scores of friends who were also in the same business or were professional people, and they formed an elite group. The furnishings in the houses in which we lived were quite different from the one that I had grown up with in Elmina and even from those of some of the kids I went to school with. People lived in clean, simple houses but my father put great emphasis on color and taste. My half-brother, sisters and I were put through a rigorous drill of elocution and deportment. While walking through the yard, we would be stopped and told "Now that you are wearing shorts or informal clothes you can walk like that, but just think how clumsy you'd look if you had a suit on."

Everything had to be so correct and proper that at school I tended to expect my mates to be just like me. I failed to understand why some of the kids still exhibited what to me appeared to be bad manners. I could talk with the other kids and play with them but because of my "snooty" ways I was never able to develop deep, long-lasting friendships.

Except when he drank soup my father had no use for cutlery, but because he wanted us to be introduced to the so-called art of good living he insisted that we the children take turns in setting the table. I learned to differentiate soup plates from a flat plate; wine glasses from water glasses. My whole orientation into the Western world had begun. I was gradually leaving the typical African world I had been born into.

To qualify for my diploma in journalism I had to spend eighteen months in the field, in addition to the theoretical experience I had already acquired. Radio

Ghana to which I was initially attached was very uneventful. I covered some bland, uninteresting assignments like the meeting of the local Red Cross, Distillers Association meetings, and a few more stories of that kind. Then I joined the Ghana Information Services which I think was a big break not only in my career, but also in my social life, and in what I had set out to achieve considering my orientation into Western society. I was made an assistant to the Press Liaison Officer, a job that constantly brought me in touch with foreign correspondents from Britain, the U.S., Poland, Yugoslavia, U.S.S.R., Germany, and Switzerland. Some of these correspondents became very close friends. From them I learned more and more about the world beyond my own. I appreciated their world more than my own. I had a better rapport with these people than I had with my own people. Looking back now, I can see that when a person reaches that stage where he sees no good in his people and their traditions, he is in serious trouble. The sad thing is that I did not know I had become a misfit in my own society partly through my own doing. I am positive that the bulk of Ghanaians and Africans—and there are millions who find themselves in the same position that I was—are not aware of that fact either.

By the time that my attachment with the Ghana Information Services was over and I had transferred to the Ghana News Agency, I had reinforced my number of White friends. I had gone beyond the foreign correspondents. I had acquired friends in almost half of the diplomatic community. I was, however, so naive and immature that it did not occur to me that by assigning me regularly to the diplomatic beat, the Agency knew exactly what it was doing. I found out one day when I went into the office, checked the assignment roster and discovered that for the sixth time in succession I had, in addition to my morning assignments, to cover another national day reception. I flared up and walked up to the News Editor.

He expected that reaction. He was smiling when I got to his desk, but for once that smile failed to seduce me.

"Van" I shouted, "I don't appreciate this one bit and you know it. There are several reporters here who are dying to cover national day receptions because of the free booze. I don't even drink and you're always putting me on this beat."

"Kwesi" he explained, "You know many of the people there. It's easy for you to carry on any conversation with them and bring us a story. Besides you send someone who drinks and no story ever reaches us."

"I see."

My education, training and associations had so confused me that on my arrival in the U.S. in 1968, I was what America calls "an Oreo cookie," a Black man with a White mentality. I was what Fanon described as a "Black face with a White mask." In short, I was mixed-up, someone who knew his roots but because of his upbringing and education, looked down on his roots and behaved as if he were of a different cultural fiber.

My mother is a strict woman who believes that children should be given responsibilities from an early age. My father was a strong disciplinarian too, but where my mother gave affection where affection was needed and disciplined mercilessly if she decided a child needed discipline, my father was different. He believed, as do most Ghanaian fathers his age, that if you allowed a child to see how you felt about him the child took advantage of your love. He became undisciplined and hard to control. There should always be a certain amount of distance and fear between fathers and children. This explains why many Ghanaian children are much closer to their mothers than to their fathers, and also why any time a Ghanaian youth finds himself in any trouble he confides first in his mother. She in turn wakes up her husband in the early hours of the morning to discuss the trouble with him. It is generally believed among Ghanaians that the early hours of the morning are the most suitable time for married people to discuss their quarrels and for favors to be asked from friends.

My father believed that children should be sheltered. He felt that a child who sees too much and hears too much, ends up talking too much. If we were in the house and heard any noise outside that attracted attention, we were forbidden to run out to see what had happened. Out of the thousand onlookers, my father said, you may be the only one to be picked to bear testimony of the incident.

Six years after my joining the Ghana Foreign Service, I was posted to the Ghana Embassy in Washington,

D.C., as Information Officer. By accepting the job, I broke away from the shelter I had been used to. And, just as my father feared, I have seen too much in America, I have heard too much. The only thing I am not doing is talking too much.

Traditionally, Foreign Service officers around the world have kept their eyes and ears open, and their mouths closed. I have never considered myself a crusader, but I can no longer keep my lips shut. What right do I have to expect that someone else should correct the things that I think are unjust?

America has been a turning point in my life. Mentally and politically, America has helped me tremendously to grow up. It is the observations, experiences and fears that have helped me to mature that I now share with other peoples of the world, especially Americans—both Black and White—and Africans.

1

All That Glitters is Not Gold

(Old English Proverb)

Two days after my arrival in Washington to assume duty as Information Officer for the Ghana Embassy in Washington, I was asked to proceed to New York to help with the press coverage of our delegation to the United Nations. My ears still ached a little from the fourteen-hour direct flight between Accra, Ghana's capital, and Washington, so I chose to go to New York by bus. The thought of going to New York and living there for a time was like a dream come true. To many young Ghanaians, New York, Chicago and Los Angeles are the cities that make up America. Any Ghanaian returning home is peppered with questions about these cities. If it becomes evident that he has visited none of them, he is teased and told he didn't really see America.

From all the bits and pieces I had read and heard,

New York was "fun city." As a fun-loving person myself, I greatly looked forward to the experience of living there.

At five o'clock on a Sunday in September, I walked onto the platform at the bus terminal, retrieved my two suitcases, and got my carry-all, which I hung over my shoulder.

Within five minutes of my arrival, I was undergoing my first cultural shock in America. The heat was suffocating! All I wore on top of my pants was a light African shirt (call it "Dashiki" if you want), but the armpits were dripping with sweat. I had left Africa only two days before. I had heard and read of foreigners complaining bitterly about the intense heat in Africa. Quite naturally, I had come to America thinking that such intensity could not be felt anywhere outside the tropics. Ghana's eighty-five degrees all the year round was sometimes uncomfortable and sticky, but New York's heat seemed to break every fiber in me.

I was afraid I would collapse if I stayed at that terminal for any length of time. I wanted to get out of there fast, but there was no sign of the officer from our New York office who had been detailed to meet me and check me into a hotel.

I thought he was probably mixed up somewhere in the crowd. It seemed as though all of New York City must be at the terminal—young and old, Black and White, civilians and servicemen, drunk and sober, dudes and hippies. They were all there. I had underestimated the size of the terminal. The huge size of the crowd, their restless activities, and the buses which seemed to be coming in every two seconds, were all too much for my senses to take.

Suddenly, I realized that my bus had been delayed an hour. Probably our man in New York had given me up entirely. Staying at the terminal longer, I concluded, would not be advisable. I would have to find my own way to the Ghana Consulate on Fifth Avenue. Then I remembered that I had left Washington without asking for the address of the Consulate. I lifted each suitcase with one arm and started to look for help.

Naive as I was, I kept hoping that someone in the crowd would kindly relieve me of one of my suitcases. I thought what held in Ghana would also hold in New York. But no one even looked at me, let alone offered to help. I had been taught in school that in Western societies men always vacate their seats in buses and in public places for women, and that it is men who carry heavy luggage. At the terminal, however, many women were carrying suitcases in one hand and pushing others with their feet. If people would not come to the rescue of a woman, what made me expect they would rescue me?

As I made my way through the crowd, several people bumped rudely into me. No one stopped. No one said "I am sorry." They just walked away as if nothing had happened. I tried to ask people for directions out of the terminal to the street, but they looked at me suspiciously and walked away. For about half an hour, I circled around the terminal, unable to make my way into the street. Again, I displayed my total ignorance of American life. I approached a man who was selling hotdogs and asked him if he would kindly keep an eye on one of my suitcases while I carried the other one into the street for a cab.

He gave me an angry look. In Ghana, it would be risky to make such a request to one of the people just sitting there, but Ghanaians who own shops and stalls in railway and bus stations are used to travellers leaving their luggage in their care.

I turned to a middle-aged Black woman who was selling subway tokens. After listening to my story, she asked her colleague to excuse her and walked with me into the street.

On our way out, I half expected she would offer to take one of the suitcases! She did not. I was so used to kindness that I was really expecting too much from people. What the lady did for me, however, was more helpful than carrying my suitcase. She led me to the street where I hailed a taxi, and even gave the cab driver the address of the Ghana Consulate.

New York immediately became a series of further shocks. Before the driver moved his cab, his meter had jumped to thirty-five cents. I could not understand how the man could charge me that kind of money before he had given any service. I opened my mouth to protest, but before I had time to do so we were already at 42nd Street and Broadway. Never in my life had I seen so many people walking in one street.

"Where are they all going?" I asked the driver.

"Just walking around," he replied.

I had seen crowds, but only at ceremonies of one kind or the other. Yet thousands of people, mostly young, dressed in blue jeans and mod clothes, paraded around Times Square and Broadway, doing absolutely nothing.

We turned into Fifth Avenue. The sidewalks were still jammed with people. Here it was not the crowds I minded. What frightened me was the skyline. I had admired skyscrapers in two West African cities, Lagos and Abidjan, which are built on islands and consequently suffer from land shortages; but the feeling I had in that cab was that New York City's skyline was closing in on me. It was a frightening feeling.

No one was at the Consulate when I got there. The driver suggested that we continue to the UN Secretariat where he thought all the member-nations maintained offices. I was a little hesitant. One of the things I had heard from Ghanaians who had lived abroad was about taxi-drivers and their tricky ways. I suspected that he knew I was not a New Yorker and might swindle me.

I had always prided myself on being extraordinarily independent, but at that moment I had such a great need for Ghanaian company that after a little hesitation, I agreed to the driver's suggestion. It turned out that the UN Secretariat was also closed on Sundays.

I gave up. Nothing mattered anymore. All I wanted was a place to sleep overnight. Just about a block or so from the UN we spotted a hotel.

The driver dropped me there. I asked for a room—

the cheapest they had, I told the receptionist. When the bellboy opened the door to the room, I gasped. It was, it seemed to me, two feet by two. My fear of heights and small spaces returned. I could not figure out how I could bear to stay a whole night in that room without suffering from nightmares—that is, if I managed to get any sleep.

I stood there, wondering whether I should ask for a different room. In the midst of my confusion, I heard the bellboy say for the umpteenth time, "I hope you like your room, Sir."

Didn't he realize that I was not in any mood for conversation? All I wanted was to be left alone. Then I remembered that back home in Ghana if someone visited his friends or family and kept announcing his departure, it was generally assumed that he needed money or was waiting for something which had been promised him.

I had only been in America for three days. I did not understand the currency. I did not know a nickel from a dime. My bills in Washington had been taken care of by the Embassy. Truthfully, I did not think the bellboy deserved a tip—all he had done was to carry the smaller of my two suitcases, leaving me to carry the heavy one and the carryall. I took some change from my pocket. The nickels looked larger than the dimes. I thought they were worth more. I gave him four. The expression on his face was not too pleasant. Now that I know the difference, I can imagine that young man swearing at the management for admitting "Niggers" to the hotel.

After about a month or so I suddenly discovered that I had been living in the city without anyone that I could call a friend. I was so used to having people around me, people calling at different hours that I thought that the situation in New York was strange. There were many Ghanaian students I had seen at the office. Some of them I had known in Ghana, but the broad, friendly smile which one associates with Ghanaians was gone. If some of the students saw you first, they avoided you. Those who were unable to avoid you or showed genuine delight in seeing you exchanged telephone numbers with you. In some instances you never heard from them again. What kind of life, I wondered, were people living in New York City? New York seemed to have molded the Ghanaians into its own image. There was nothing that I needed more than meeting some Americans and talking to them. I smiled at people. I tried to make conversation with strangers, but people looked at me suspiciously. I even discovered that the people who said "Good morning" to me when they entered the hotel elevators were all foreigners who were used to greeting strangers.

I felt so lonely and dejected that eventually I was forced into taking long, aimless walks around the city after working hours. Rockefeller Center, 42nd Street West and the stores on Fifth Avenue became my refuge.

Before taking any of my long, nocturnal walks I would always stop at one of the small, corner grocery shops which abound in the city of New York. From there I would buy a pound of grapes, peaches, plums, apples, or

31

pears. I could not believe that where I had paid a fortune for any of these fruits in Ghana, here in the U.S. I was being charged something like thirty cents or just a little more. I knew that these fruits cost very much in Ghana largely because the country is tropical. These fruits would not grow there. Like all imports they become expensive in Ghanaian stores.

To me, however, the cheap prices were part of the good life in America. As I took my nightly walks I stuffed myself with these fruits. I ate so much that I woke up each morning or in the middle of the night with a running stomach. I had no idea then that these fruits had also been heavily sprayed with disinfectant and that my failure to wash them thoroughly before eating them was to lead to a terrible throat infection that would take a year and two doctors to cure.

Sometimes I would sit in a cafeteria or restaurant for hours on end, watching people drink gallons of black coffee. Alone with my thoughts I tried to understand why Americans drank so much black coffee.

I had been accustomed to drinking and seeing people drink a cup or two of coffee a day. To obtain the maximum enjoyment from it the majority of Ghanaians would add plenty of milk and sugar to their coffee. Without these, coffee to them only has an aroma but no taste. Quite naturally what I saw the New Yorkers drink in the restaurant on my way to the office each morning seemed like diluted mud. By the time that I finally got settled in my own apartment in Washington and started to entertain, I had learned that no meal in America was complete without coffee. I served coffee to my American friends after every meal. The strange thing was that these friends either ignored the coffee or took a sip and left their cups of coffee to get cold. It took me three years to discover that my friends were just too nice and polite to point out that I perhaps brewed the worst coffee in the U.S. It was the teenage son of friends of mine who had come to stay with me on his vacation who said, "Fred, this is no coffee at all. It's so watery it tastes like . . ." "Be quiet," I interrupted, but I was glad he had solved the puzzle for me.

I was also amazed at the amount of ice that the Americans used. It annoyed me to see the waitresses fill half the cup of the coke or other sodas I had ordered with cracked ice. That really left me with no soda at all.

Certain words and phrases began to puzzle me. I wondered why in restaurants the lunches that I ordered were always referred to as dinners. I could be in a restaurant around one o'clock eating lunch, but the waitresses always screamed into the intercom "One chicken dinner." After the meal, the question was always the same wherever I went: "Ready for your check?" Until I learned that they meant a bill and not a bank cheque, I was very confused. I had had their services. If anyone should write a cheque it was I, so why did they always ask if I was ready for my check?

In Elmina no one ever counts money into anyone's hands. The theory is that such action impoverishes the person into whose hands the money is being dropped. In New York, every restaurant cashier and every store assistant counted the money into my hands. How, I asked, could I make these people understand, without their considering me superstitious, that one simply does not do that? I think I now understand why I failed to save any money during the period of my assignment in America. I also wondered why everyone seemed to hand me things with the left hand. In Ghanaian society this is considered most disrespectful but in New York people did so without blinking their eyes. I learned that the New Yorkers did not mean to insult me. It was just that I was dealing with people of a different cultural background.

After leaving the restaurant, I would walk to 42nd Street West to satisfy myself that some of the things I had seen the previous nights were real and had not been imagined. Forty-second Street and Broadway were for me the greatest entertainment. From Broadway I would continue to Rockefeller Plaza where I would watch the ice skaters for a while.

Gradually I became close to some of the Ghanaian students. In my discussions with them I came to realize that quite a few of them, especially those who had resident visas, had no intention whatsoever of returning home. Some of these were private students who had come to America through their own efforts and had, through hard work, put themselves through school. There were also those whose education in the U.S. had been paid for by the Ghanaian government. I felt quite strongly that these students, especially those sponsored by the Ghana government, should return to Ghana not only because they had an obligation to do so but also because a developing country like ours can utilize all kinds of skills.

I came to realize, after some time, that even though I disapproved of the extension of stay of Ghanians in the U.S., there were some admissions that I had to make to myself. Many of the Ghanaians had a better life in America. Salaries, for instance, were very high. Those who had qualified and had chosen to stay were in some cases making as much as three to four times the salaries that their colleagues in Ghana were making. It is true that they did not live in fashionable or middle class neighborhoods, but the housing, in many instances, was adequate and furnished with labor-saving devices which cost a fortune back in Ghana. I became proud of the students. Some had more than one job. It was hard on them. They were not used to the efficiency and the hard work of the American people, but if they had to put themselves through school, they had little choice.

I saw the students walk through severe weather conditions that they were not used to, to go to work. Where in developing Africa could one combine work and study and find time for an occasional entertainment? Where in developing Africa, which still maintains the educational system left by the French and the British, could a student drop out of school, save up and return a semester or two later without loss of credits? Where in developing Africa could a student afford the cost of an automobile?

It dawned on me that in addition to what I had learned about America from various American friends I had known in Ghana, there were still quite a few remarkable things I had to learn on my own. I followed with great interest and admiration America's democratic machinery. The fact that someone could express a dissenting view from the one held by the administration even though he himself is a member of the party in power, was for me a novelty; the fact that any American could make his views known on any subject without fear of being penalized astounded me. I also admired the extent of freedom of the press, although there were certain things that the newspapers published that I thought constituted a threat to personal and national security.

I had left Ghana at a time that one could describe as "depression." Stores were virtually empty. Prices of goods were astronomical. I could not believe that in the U.S. there were strings of department stores and shops. Not only were these stores and shops fully stocked with one's needs and wants, they had variety. What was more, they made it easy for you to obtain your requirements by way of credit.

In late November I came down with the flu. Everyone was describing it as the Hong Kong flu, though I never quite understood why it had been so labeled. I was miserable. For a whole night I burned with fever. My condition was so bad that for a while I feared I was going to die. Suddenly I remembered that I had in my hotel room an instrument that I should have thought of using before to get help but had completely forgotten, the telephone.

Not very many people in Ghana could privately afford a telephone. I grabbed the receiver. Seconds later an answer came. "May I help you?"

Before I could answer I started to throw up. In a few minutes, the manager of the hotel and another person had let themselves into my room with the spare key. I thought that they were going to move me to a hospital. They did not. Rather, they summoned a doctor. Coming from a country where medical facilities are not half as developed and where there is one doctor for at least 10,000 people, I could not help being impressed by such efficient medical attention as the one I had just received or the great number of well-equipped hospitals and specialists I was later to see across the entire country.

Prior to my arrival in the U.S. I had seen America only in films and magazines. I had joined my friends and thousands of other Ghanaians in saying that the people who really live well are the Americans, the Europeans and the British. They live in big houses, drive flashy cars. Our feelings were of self pity. Now I was seeing all this with my own eyes.

In the second month of my stay in New York, I was invited to dinner in a home in suburban New York. After a delicious meal, the hostess asked me to retire to the living room. I did, and a few minutes later she joined me. The two of us began a discussion on Africa. Her fourteen-year-old son walked in, sat at the piano and started to play. From where I sat in the living room I could see the father put on an apron and start working on the dishes.

What a cultural shock! A man doing the dishes while

his fourteen-year-old boy played the piano? I could not see myself or any other Ghanaian boy that age being so pampered. If any of our neighbors or relatives had come into our house and seen such an incident, they surely would have wanted to find out who ruled that house, and what kind of training my parents were giving me. Even my elder brothers would not do the dishes while I entertained myself.

Every young man or woman who lives at home with his parents has certain household chores to perform. These may include washing and ironing the parents' clothes, polishing shoes, polishing floors, washing the car if there is one in the family, marketing and cooking.

My job as Information Officer brought me into personal contact with thousands of young people from grade school to college. Junior and senior high school students often asked me what young people their own age in Ghana would do from day to day. When I told them, they grinned. In the words of one Black Washington high school boy, what I had told him about the chores of a boy in Ghana sounded like "a lot of trash." A White boy from Delaware said, "Sounds like slavery to me."

I was dealing with people from a different cultural background, so I did not expect them to see eye to eye with me on this subject. What disturbed me, however, was what appeared to be the extreme rudeness of many American high school boys and girls.

I felt greatly embarrassed hearing certain statements that some teenagers made to their own parents or teachers. The interesting thing was that the parents and teachers did not seem as upset as I was about what had been said or if they were, their faces did not betray them. I now concede that the scope which American parents allow their children have helped American young people to develop a great deal of self-confidence, outspokenness and views on major domestic and international issues. Such self-confidence and outspokenness I had lacked while I was in school. I cannot think of more than a dozen people in my class or the other classes who possessed these qualities since the relationship between ourselves and our parents was such that words must be carefully weighed before they were uttered. Very few Ghanaian children ever enter into discussions on various subjects with their parents. Children who show interest in adult conversation are severely warned not to allow themselves to be caught showing such interest again. A child who always shows interest in adult conversation gives an indication that he would grow up to be a liar, they contended. I am inclined to think that the American way of bringing up children is perhaps the best and most suitable for child development as against the Ghanaian way, which is archaic in today's world.

My own relationship with people had not improved. I was still lonely. There were certain things I had seen about people in New York that to me as a foreigner did not make sense. Still, New York remained unique. I had never seen anything so huge, so complex, so crowded, so fast, so dirty and yet so irresistible. But just about the time that I was becoming engrossed in America's great advancements, a few things happened that made me compare myself to a boy from rural America who had heard so much about the city and against great odds had saved every penny he could lay his hands on. Eventually he had his chance, and moved to the city. He was dazzled by the great neon lights, the push-button service, the efficiency of the people—indeed, all that he had dreamed the great city would be. However, he also saw and experienced a great many things which disagreed so much with his own cultural background and principles that he said to himself "If this is what it is all about, I don't want any part of it." He talked about his experiences. He could not conceal his bitter frustration. The city folks who were used to the city life resented this peasant criticizing their way of life. He told them he was not criticizing. Rather he thought that by sharing his experiences with them they could stop somewhere and take a closer look at themselves.

That peasant is me. My city is America.

My biggest disappointment occurred the day I found a man spitting phlegm on Fifth Avenue. Spitting in the streets of the White man's country? I could not believe it! I wished all the teachers who had taught me hygiene in school could have been present at the scene. It was a sight that no Ghanaian would expect to see anywhere in Europe or America. Instantly, I remembered the joke which many Ghanaian parents and children share. Ghanaian children, on learning hygiene at school, become so critical of their elders' habits that they never stop pointing out that "This is dirty. That is unclean." Sometimes this becomes so overbearing that the person who is being corrected retorts: "Leave me alone. Hygeia's mother was killed by germs." In other words, if the goddess of hygiene was so perfect her mother would not have died of germs.

But if that little incident shocked me I was soon to discover something that has led me to conclude that whether we admit it or not, no nation can be spiritually the same after years of technological and industrial development.

I was taught this lesson very forcefully one day in a cafeteria at 47th Street and Fifth Avenue.

I had gone there with a Ghanaian girl working in the Consulate. She had been in the U.S. longer than I had. As we sat down to eat our meal, we heard what sounded like vomiting. We turned around. Sure enough, a man had been taken violently sick. There were at least a hundred people in the room. Everyone simply pretended he had not seen what was happening. I jumped, but before I could leave my chair my companion grabbed me. "Where do you think you're going?" she asked me.

"To help that man," I answered.

"No, you don't. This is not Ghana. Here everyone minds his own business."

"But the man is ill," I protested, as the people around us looked on.

"You're only asking for trouble, Kwesi. Sit down," the girl ordered.

A man could have been dying. In the name of minding our own business, we watched in silence. In Ghana, women would have screamed, and men would have rushed to his assistance.

What struck me as equally odd was how my companion had so quickly shed her own human values and replaced them with what pertains in New York City. It was a sad day for me. I prayed that I should never be a witness to such an incident again.

The unhappy incident at the cafeteria was still fresh in my mind when I ran into another problem which further opened my eyes about American society. This time the incident involved me.

One Saturday morning, I left my hotel room to go to the desk to check for mail. I took from my suitcase a pair of new Ghanaian sandals which I had received as a present from a friend. I did not realize until I reached the lobby and started to walk on the uncarpeted terrazo floors that the sandals were too slippery and definitely unsuitable for bare floors. I feared that I would slip any moment. Just as I reached the desk, it happened. I slipped, but steadied myself before I could lose my balance. What I could not understand was the contrast between the indifference of the residents who were sitting in the lobby, and the over-concern of four employees of the hotel, who rushed out to see me.

Gradually, the story behind it began to unfold. The manager feared that if I had slipped and broken an arm or leg, I would have brought a law suit against the management. To me, this was nonsense. If I had been injured no one would have been blamed but myself.

When I narrated the story to some friends of mine, they thought I was a fool. I should have lowered my body to the ground, pulled a face, and complained of pain in some part of my body, they explained.

After this I understood the meaning of a sign which not only seemed to follow me wherever I went, but from then on annoyed me as well. The elevator operator said each time I got on at my floor, "Watch your step." Before entering a bus, the same sign was visible. If it rained or snowed, there was a whole parade of "Watch your step" signs in the city of New York. I was told that this was to avoid accidents which might involve hotels, stores, offices and property owners in law suits. The whole thing did not make sense to me. It was unfortunate if someone fell, but to try to claim damages because of an accident that was not caused by anyone to me sounded wicked.

I chided people I knew who would cross streets casually in front of moving cars. They assumed the drivers would not knock them down. If the drivers did knock them down they were assured of a little fortune arising out of that accident. I have not yet been able to fathom how lives could be equated with money.

My mother, as indicated earlier, is a simple, down-to-earth woman like many of the people from Elmina. In one of her visits to Accra to see me, she expressed the desire to see a film. To get to the theater we had to walk past Ghana's first fountain erected after independence. On seeing the fountain my mother could not help admiring it. She then asked me what that display of water was for. I told her it was part of the plan to make the city beautiful. "Your city beautiful!" she said, shocked. "Some people in this country can't get any clean water to drink. They have to walk miles to a river. And here you are with so much to drink that you can even afford to waste some."

At that time I did not share my mother's lack of enthusiasm for the fountain. Ghana was a young nation, striving for progress. Progress, in my estimation then, should include all the impressive things that Europe and America had. That some parts of the country did not have a clean water supply was unimportant. What was important was that the city of Accra, Ghana's capital, should be made a showplace.

After my American experience, I have come to appreciate more and more my mother's philosophy that both the government and society cannot allow a situation in which some have an overabundance of the things which others have been denied.

It was in Houston's famous Astrodome that I began to recall what my mother had said to me six years before. I had been shocked at the cost of the mammoth structure. It was a remarkable example of architecture. It had brought fame to the city. But I still could not forget the many poor people I had seen in Houston, Austin, San Antonio and Dallas. The poor living conditions of the Black and Mexican population in these areas sharply reduced my admiration for the splendor of the mammoth Astro-dome. Would the money not have been better used in improving the lot of the poor?

This negative attitude of mine toward what others may term progress again came to mind during my tour of the Los Angeles Arts Complex and a new ultra-modern Catholic church in San Francisco, estimated to have cost a hundred million dollars. Initially, I was deeply impressed by the crushed velvet draperies, Belgian chandeliers and thick, rich, ruby-red carpets that adorn the Los Angeles theaters, but thoughts of human misery elsewhere soon made me wonder if such luxury was necessary. In San Francisco, I thought the church was guilty of a grievous sin.

I became impatient with the Ghanaian community. I could not understand why they always stuck together and would not mingle with the Americans as a way of broadening their own horizons. Soon it became evident that their reason for sticking together was not that they wanted to be around each other all the time.

Meaningful friendship with Americans are few and far between. Americans I found basically as friendly as Ghanaians. But they are so caught up in making money for taxes, medical and legal bills and keeping up with the Joneses that they have little time for the friendship that the Ghanaians seek when they try to break away from their own group.

The Americans mean well, but unless a foreigner understands their problems he ends up thinking that they are an unfriendly people.

Throughout my life I have met thousands of people that I have no desire to see again, but irrespective of my personal feelings about these people I still believe in the Ghanaian philosophy that "people are sweet." We have our own human jealousies, greed and dislike of people without causes, but we also realize that there are very few things we can do without others. In a highly-industrialized country like the U.S. this beautiful human dependence on others has been destroyed to such an extent that one's sincere concern for others seems to irritate the very people for whom such concern is shown.

You hear of a friend's misfortune. You express profound sorrow. You are told "Please don't try to carry my burden." What is friendship for? I wondered. I was distressed to see so many people who had offered unsolicited advice being thanked politely for not minding their own business. Back in Ghana I would have cause to tell a friend "You have your troubles and I have mine" only when he rushes to me each time he has a problem but refuses to take the advice I give. I shall never give anyone the impression that I was so burdened with my own problems that I could not be bothered to listen to his.

In America I found that people are even afraid to tell others about their problems because they will be rebuffed. This is why day and night I pray to whoever is supposed to have this whole wretched earth in His hands to guide my own people in Ghana in such a way that in their quest for economic and technological progress they strive also to maintain their human values. Without it, their society will be like a house without a foundation.

+   +   +

The time in New York passed swiftly, and I began to be acclimated to my new city. Soon I had been in New York for two months, and I still had not seen the famous Harlem. Deep down in my heart, the desire to see Harlem was almost more than I could control. From the reports that one read and heard, however, one went to Harlem at one's own risk. I didn't know what to believe.

One morning my former boss in Accra, who also happened to be on the Ghana delegation to the UN, asked me to go with him to Broadway to buy records. During our shopping trip he asked if I had been to the Apollo Theater to hear any of the Black singers. When I told him that not only had I not gone to the Apollo, but that I was afraid to walk through the streets of Harlem, his face showed genuine surprise. "You're probably safer in Harlem than you are on the streets of Manhattan," he said.

Whether he was being facetious or not I didn't know. But after what he said, I resolved I was no longer going to let my own fears intimidate me. Whatever happened, I was going to Harlem!

On my arrival at the subway station at 42nd Street and 7th Avenue that Saturday, the dread that I had developed for riding the subway came back in a rush. Nothing was as confusing to me as trying to follow directions at subway stations.

47

I was always ready to ask for new directions as soon as whoever was giving them was through. "Follow the I.R.T. signs. Stand on the platform to your right. Take the E train to 59th Street. Change for the F train to Ely. Walk down to the basement platform, and take the A train. You can't miss it." Can't miss it, indeed!

I went through the same drill again that Saturday. In between stations, the fear that I might miss my stops and changes weighed heavily on my mind.

Next to me on the seat sat a huge, six-foot Black man who seemed friendly enough. It occurred to me that I could ask him for help—"How does one get to Harlem from here?" I decided against it. The minute he detected my accent, he was going to ask me where I came from. This would turn into a conversation with all eyes of the other passengers on me.

The situation, however, was becoming critical. The train was traveling at a speed which seemed faster than sound. Any moment it could be too late—I would learn I should have already changed trains somewhere or that I had missed my stop. Reluctantly, I turned to the six-footer.

Just as I had feared, he detected an accent, but it fooled him! "What's the matter with you folks? Go to college, come back acting uppity like White folks. Shoot! Don't know where Harlem is eh, sonny?"

While he was continuing with his outburst, a man who was sitting a little distance from us, and who had apparently heard my question, told me I had to get off at the same stop he was to make. Then he cautioned, "If you should lose your way, don't talk to nobody. Just wait till you see a police officer or a mailman." That scared me. Harlem, I was becoming convinced now, must be a pretty dangerous place to hang around.

I followed the steps upward. In a few minutes I was out on 125th Street and St. Nicholas Avenue. At first sight, Harlem was pitiful. Shrouded by the dull, grey skies of late fall, the streets of Harlem looked deserted. Along the pavements stood rows of garbage cans, some overflowing. Hungry-looking dogs struggled to bring the cans down. On stoops sat unshaved men wearing hats—obviously they had been at the bottle all night. Occasionally, a woman in slacks or a mini-dress stopped somewhere on the pavement fumbling with her cigarette while she tried to steady herself. She had had too much to drink.

The idea of Harlem being a dangerous place was still so fresh in my mind that when one of these women staggered towards me, I jumped even before she spoke: "You don't wanna do nothing, do you?" I jumped again when a drunken man sitting on a stoop smiled and said "Come here."

But the more I saw of the depressing sights and sounds of Harlem, the more I wanted to be in it. I began to feel the same attachment, sense of belonging and fear which I found unique in many poor, tough districts of West African countries.

I walked on. Soon I was in Spanish Harlem. For the first time since I had left Ghana, I felt homesick. In those shops in Spanish Harlem were many of the foodstuffs I had thought were only peculiar to Ghana—plantains, yams, casava, and root ginger.

The day went by fast. I walked back to 125th Street. I stood in front of the Apollo Theater watching the dudes and their dates arrive for the mid-afternoon show. The colors of their outfits were saucy—deep purple, green, yellow and blue silk shirts worn over the same color of pants. Over these outfits were what appeared to be expensive winter coats. On top of their neatly shaped "Afros" were little, funny-shaped hats.

I had left my country at a time when more and more Ghanaian women were spending quite a bit on straightening, bleaching and pressing their hair. Like many Ghanaian men I had admired this new trend in fashions, so quite understandably I did not take too kindly to the Black women I saw in Harlem wearing the "Afro." I had not been caught up in Black identity yet and did not understand why the American Black woman should try to develop a new image. No matter how good a woman looked in the "Afro," my mind was closed. But if I came across Black men who had had their hair processed, I felt like running through it all with a sharp scissors!

Later I was also amazed in Harlem at the number of men's fashions and beads said to be African although I had not seen such things anywhere in Africa. Some of these things just irked me. Somehow I expected that I should gain more acceptance from the Blacks in New York. When this did not happen, I became a little doubtful about the whole question of Black identity with Africa and how sincere its advocates are. Perhaps it is this feeling that Americans describe as "thinking someone owes you something."

Not too long after the Harlem visit, I met the Kirkaldys, a Black family in Queens that I now claim and feel a part of. Before our meeting, I still was not convinced that Blacks in America were an oppressed people, and that they were denied decent jobs, housing and education. I had read of segregation in the South, the use of police dogs, Little Rock, Martin Luther King, and the riots. But I never believed that the situation could be as bad as some Blacks I had talked to had said. I could not see how anyone could have such hate in his heart as to draw a gun at the sight of a Black person. My mind believed what it had been made to believe from reading and talking to some White Americans—that the Negro was underprivileged because he was lazy.

The Kirkaldys had invited me to stay with them one weekend. I was on my way when an incident happened which opened my eyes for the first time to the strained relations between America's Black and White people.

The F train to Queens was crowded as it is during any evening rush hour. Riders were crushed against each other. At Queens Plaza many of the passengers disembarked, but the seats were still fully occupied. I spotted a vacant seat and pointed it out to a Black woman standing next to me, who was fully laden with packages.

As she moved toward the seat, a White woman sitting

there spread her legs wide to prevent the other from taking the seat. The Black woman landed on the lap of the White woman, and refused to move until the White woman made room for her. This incident took me by surprise.

The night before this happened, alone in my hotel room I had seen on television a debate on the Black Panther Party between Eldridge Cleaver and the conservative columnist, William Buckley. That debate offered me my first insight into the Black Panther movement and its objectives. By nature, I have always been strongly opposed to violence. My education had also made me partial to Whites. Quite naturally, some of the statements that Mr. Cleaver made troubled me. I saw America at that time as a country that belonged rightfully to the White community. Progress for the Blacks, I had managed to convince myself, should come gradually and they had no right to threaten the peace and security of the White community.

After that experience in the subway, it dawned on me that perhaps I had been too harsh in my estimation of the Blacks. I had come to America believing what I had heard: that the American Negro had been left out of the mainstream of the economy, education, housing and jobs solely on account of his own laziness and inability to produce. I had allowed my already prejudiced mind to jump to conclusions without opening my eyes and my mind. I learned that evening that hate and prejudice surely do exist somewhere.

The following Saturday, I went on a shopping trip on

Fifth Avenue. Around noon, I entered a department store at 35th Street. On the right-hand side of the first floor was the menswear department. Some of the clothes displayed there attracted my attention, and I walked towards the counter. It was late fall. I was experiencing my first spell of cold weather, and my thumbs and fingers were numb. I had my hands in the pockets of my outer coat.

I bent over so that I would have a good view of the clothes. Suddenly it hit me that someone behind me was in step with me. If I took two steps, he did exactly the same. If I stopped he stopped too. The thought occurred that whoever was following me was a pickpocket and that I should be careful of my movements. Then I remembered that I was not carrying much, and there were so many people in the store that no one could possibly be so brazen as to carry out such a theft.

I turned sharply. Our eyes met. I recognized him immediately—a security officer for the store. I know that each store had its security men to prevent and minimize theft, but why was I so suspicious looking that I had to be followed so closely? The hurt was deep. I learned for the first time that each time a young Black enters a store he makes the people there nervous.

What immediately entered my mind was that the security officer had done this for only one reason: I was Black. There I was, living in New York for three months under an assumption that I was different—an African, and therefore an untouchable. Not like American Blacks.

My mind raced back to a poem I had read in Ghana
University's publication a year before:

Give me a Soul

Because I am Black

But too White within

To have a Soul.

I was learning fast that this fabled land of milk and
honey had a few flies in the cream pitcher. But in a
strange land where no one seemed to trust me because of
my skin color, at least there was one place that would be a
haven of peace and fellowship, I was sure—my church.

2

In My Father's House There Will Be No Crying

(Edwin Hawkins Singers)

St. Patrick's Cathedral on New York's prestigious Fifth Avenue is an imposing, solid structure. As you enter its foyer, you see a sign conspicuously displayed for the benefit of its worshippers and for the numerous tourists who, it seems to me, diminish the sacred atmosphere. It says: "Do not enter unless you are properly dressed." I was horrified when I saw it. For five minutes I stood in the foyer, trying to figure out whether the sport shirt that I was wearing could pass for "properly dressed." I had gone to St. Patrick's on a Saturday afternoon. As far as I was concerned, I was properly dressed, but the decision did not seem to be mine to make. It was the prerogative of the cathedral administrator. If he or any of his staff saw me they could accuse me of improper dress and throw me out of the cathedral. If there was one place that I least wished to be thrown out of, it was a church.

Why would a church, of all places, put out a sign like that? I had been brought up to believe that the house of God was a place that one took one's troubles to. It was a clean heart that mattered, not the clothes that one wore. I knew back in Ghana that if anyone, women especially, wore to church clothes that were considered provocative, they became the subject of gossip and discussion. But nowhere had I seen a sign like the one at St. Patrick's.

After I had recovered from my initial shock, I surmised that the objective must be to discourage so-called hippie-looking youths from the church since their presence there might have already drawn complaints from some of the parishioners. I saw the parish's point of view, but on second thought, I asked whether St. Patrick's was not guilty of the very things that Christ himself spoke against. I thought of so many references in the Bible to this effect—the Jews who paid devout attention to the cleanliness of the body; of Mary Magdalene anointing Christ with oil and the reaction from the people; of Christ socializing with public sinners and again the reaction of the people. Is it not important that a young person in the midst of a revolt against materialism still finds time to communicate with God? A large proportion of the well-dressed "proper" congregation might be nothing more than fornicators, adulterers, drunks and thieves behind doors. The impression one gets is that so long as one can sin in private, one cannot be accused of immorality.

These thoughts also led me, for the first time, to look at the youth revolution in America from an entirely different perspective. Back in Ghana, I had never really understood what American youths were up in arms against. I strongly supported American involvement in Southeast Asia. America, I felt, should keep Communism in check. Everytime I heard of demonstrations against the government of the U.S. for its Vietnam policy, I was angered. I even agreed that the organizers of these demonstrations were in league with the Communists.

What irritated me most was the youth revolution against materialism and public morality. There we were in Africa, working as hard as we were able to try to raise our standards to live like the Americans, and there were the American youth trying to make the world believe that materialism was no good. My friends and I discussed the issue. We saw the truth in our people's philosophy "Those who have it don't want it. And those who want it can't have it."

It took a little, one-line sign at St. Patrick's Cathedral to make me see what American youths were talking about.

But regulations are regulations, so the Sunday after my visit, I decided to wear a regular suit and tie to mass. As I prepared to leave my hotel for the church, I remembered that one of the things the priests at the Catholic high school I had attended had always hammered into our heads was the need to be at mass from the very beginning. They explained that since at the beginning of each mass the celebrant asks God to absolve the congregation from its sins, it was important that Catholics should be present at that time. Between me and some of my closest friends, we agreed that to make a confession to the priest privately could sometimes be agonizing. If we could obtain forgiveness without a private confession, why should we not spare ourselves that agony?

Ever since then I have never been late to a mass. If I were late to one mass I would rather stay away and attend the later one. In light of this, I entered St. Patrick's thirty minutes before the mass was due to start. The cathedral was almost empty but the pews were gradually taken at a rate that surprised me. Within half an hour, the cathedral was filled. With the exception of the pew I occupied, all were fully taken. Some of them, I even thought, had more people than they were originally intended to take.

I wondered why people were looking for places to sit when I had a whole pew to myself. As the mass gathered momentum, more people arrived. These had no alternative but to come into the pew that I occupied. Their behavior, however, astounded me. They were keeping me at a distance.

Since childhood my parents, like all other Ghanaian parents, had impressed upon me the need for me to take two baths a day, one in the morning and another before bedtime. At nineteen I revolted against this, arguing that there was no need for a single person going to bed all by himself to take a bath in the evening. In New York during the fall my skin began to get dry and itchy. I was told by friends I did not need any soap on my skin, but I could not see how I could be clean without soaping the body thor-

58

oughly every day. On my arrival at St. Patrick's I knew one thing for sure. I was clean. I did not smell. Why was it that the other worshippers either kept me at a distance or avoided me?

The situation did not improve the Sunday following that. I decided against coming to any conclusions. The Sunday after, I had grown tired of a suit and tie. I wore my colorful "Kente" cloth to St. Patrick's. The effect was incredible. It seemed like the whole of St. Patrick's was suddenly noticing me. Something that could never happen in any Ghanaian Catholic church happened at St. Patrick's. Without any inhibition whatsoever, people walked up to me, touched my "Kente" cloth and exclaimed "Well, if that isn't beautiful," or "Oh, that is gorgeous." The attention was becoming unbearable. If I thought I could escape from all that attention after the mass was over, I was deceived. I knew that some of the people who were so full of admiration had seen me before in that church. They had not only ignored me, they had refused to sit in the same pew with me!

On my return to Washington, I registered at the Shrine of the Blessed Sacrament in the fashionable, wealthy Chevy Chase area. According to regulations that exist within the Archdiocese, no Catholic can leave his own neighborhood and register in another one.

The attitudes of the congregation of the Shrine of the Blessed Sacrament, I was soon to learn, were no different from what I had experienced at St. Patrick's. If anything, Blessed Sacrament was worse. St. Patrick's, at least, had a congregation coming from different backgrounds—the very wealthy, middle class, and a negligible percentage of the working class. Blessed Sacrament was all middle class. The congregation was very "uppity."

I thought I should quit going to church but as a Catholic, my mind had been programmed into thinking that Sunday without mass amounted to neglect of the soul and my obligations as a Catholic. Besides, I pointed out to myself, one does not go to church to socialize with the other worshippers. If the people did not want to be bothered with me, that was no reason why I should leave the church.

The "Sign of Peace," a new innovation, was introduced into the Church's ritual at this time. This ceremony, which involved the congregation offering each other a sign of peace through handshakes, preceded Holy Communion. Since I always took the first seat in any pew, it meant that after I had been offered the sign by the priest walking down the aisle, I also had to offer the sign to the person next to me. My pew was almost always empty, so that on days that the sign was offered by the priest himself, I had nothing to worry about. The trouble came on days that the celebrant says "let us now offer each other the sign of peace" and leaves the congregation to themselves. This meant that someone in the pew before me had to shake my hand or I had to show a similar gesture to someone in the pew after me or with me in the pew.

It was a short, simple gesture, one that should not

cause any problem. But as I offered my hand people pretended they did not see me. If our eyes caught each other then their expression become sheepish as if to say: "You really don't expect me to shake hands with you, do you?" After two such instances, I gave up. Why does a Black person have to work so hard at gaining acceptance? Acceptance, I thought, should be mutual. If people made it conspicuous that they did not need you, it seems to me the right thing to do is to ignore them too rather than push yourself on them.

What kind of moral and spiritual values can anyone claim when he refuses to recognize a person simply because the other person has a different color? Both the Black and White Catholic is asked at one point in his life: "Who made you?" And he is taught to reply "God made me."

I once remarked to a friend that policemen patrolling my neighborhood, a solid-White area, slowed down their cars and searched me with their eyes before gathering speed as I walked from my apartment to church for the early morning mass. My friend replied: "Fred, you sound like someone with an overworked mind."

Maybe, but I did see in Blessed Sacrament ushers who ignored my presence to the extent that they passed by me and the envelopes I waited to drop in the collection basket. Mine may have been only a "widow's mite," but they had an obligation to take it.

Blessed Sacrament also adheres strictly to protocol. Except for those who enter the church before the mass begins, it insures that most of its worshippers are duly escorted to their pews. The ushers apparently knew the habits and the dislikes of their congregation.

As was to be expected, the church was crowded on Easter Sunday. I sat down in my pew, watching the ushers lead people into seats already crowded. Just before the Gospel, one of the ushers approached me with "Move over." "At last," I thought to myself, but as I moved to make room for the people, I realized that I had been asked to move over for two Black women. The insult was obvious. I had no objection to being seated with my own people, but it was the way it was done that angered me. I was considered good enough to sit with my own people—period.

To me, that was the straw that broke the camel's back. I swore I would never set foot in Blessed Sacrament again, and I never did. The interesting thing about Blessed Sacrament was that two weeks after I left it, a group of young people walked into the church, interrupted the mass, and in a statement read over the microphone, accused the church not only of racism but also of not taking a positive attitude in the fight against racism.

My encounters with Whites in New York's St. Patrick's and Washington's Blessed Sacrament did not deter me from remaining a Catholic. I was convinced that not all Whites were the same way. I kept looking for a new parish.

I discovered that St. Ann should actually have been my parish. It was only six blocks away from my apartment and was therefore within walking distance. It also had some features which were rather unusual. Its walls, unlike those of many Catholic churches, were bare. It had its share of stained glass windows and the usual line-up of the Stations of Cross. Beyond these, it looked financially impoverished. Attendance at mass was comparatively poor.

The church was located in a middle class neighborhood, but the priests were always complaining of how the parish was unable to meet the rising costs of heating and air conditioning. One priest sarcastically remarked one Sunday that some of his congregation owned summer cottages in the country and wore fur coats in spring and fall, but dropped change into the collection.

On a cold wintry day, I walked up the steps leading to the rectory at St. Ann's to register. Over my suit was a brown imitation-leather overcoat. I wore no gloves. My fingers were freezing, so I kept them in my pocket until I reached the entrance. I took my right hand from the pocket and rang the bell. After what seemed an eternity, a young man of about fifteen or sixteen opened the door. I tried to enter the building, but found that between me and the young man was a screen door.

"Who are you? What do you want?" he said successively in a tone that was not friendly.

"May I come in?"

"Who are you? You can't come breaking into other people's houses like that."

"Correction," I yelled at him. "If I wanted to break

into a house I wouldn't choose this one. It has nothing to steal."

"Well, then why are you so much in a hurry to get in?" he asked. "You have your hands in your pocket. I know about people like you—a beard, a leather coat and hands in your pocket."

If he had not been separated from me by the screen door, I would have hit him. As chance would have it, a priest appeared, apologized for my being kept waiting, and invited me into his office. I was so enraged I did not know where to begin. Finally, I calmed down.

We went through the process of registration. Later, I inquired from him if the parish had any youth organization I could join. He informed me that there was a group known as the Young Adults. The parish, he further explained, had no direct control over the club so I would have to make my own arrangements regarding membership. He gave me the name and telephone number of a young lady to contact—the organization's secretary. By the time I returned to my apartment, the thrill of meeting other Catholics my own age was gone. America's racial intolerance was beating me down.

The next day, however, I called the young lady. Before she answered I had come to a decision. I was going to put all my cards on the table, and I did. She was all enthusiasm until I told her I was from Africa.

"Let me put it this way," I began, "if the color of my skin is going to cause problems for your organization, I'd rather stay away."

"Well, let me be quite frank with you, Mr. Hayford. The chances are fifty-fifty. I can just go ahead and tell you the names of the people who cannot accept you. So you see, it's up to you."

It all sounded like a challenge. "Okay, I'll join," I told her.

The young lady assured me she would mail me all relevant papers for the club. I have waited two years. The papers never arrived.

These and other incidents made me begin to lose some faith and credibility in the Catholic church as an institution. I no longer worry unnecessarily if I miss mass on a Sunday. I even did a few things I would never before have dreamed of—I worshipped in Black Muslim mosques in Washington on two different occasions. I attended a service in a Jewish temple in Toledo, Ohio, and joined them in prayer. I went to a Unitarian Service in New York, and worshipped with Mormons in Salt Lake City.

I was not in search of a new faith. I did this because I had come to the conclusion that the church, as a fallible institution, had no moral right to impose any restrictions on its members to keep them from worshipping in other churches. Also I could not experience in St. Patrick, Blessed Sacrament or St. Ann's the same atmosphere of peace, repentance and sanctity that music in Ghanaian churches had made me feel. The voices of the congregation as they raised them in hymns of praise of God seemed so restrained that they lacked something. My communication with God was at its lowest ebb. Sunday masses became perfunctory.

These incidents and experiences coupled with observations that I had made about some American Catholics and about the role of the churches in Africa led me to believe that Africans who have been converted to Christianity take the religion more seriously than the Westerners themselves. I also came to the conclusion that in spite of the great pioneering work of the churches in Africa in the fields of education and medicine, one could also hold them responsible for confusing the minds of Africans with respect to religion and culture.

Like all the men and women who had gone through either missionary or government-sponsored schools since my country was colonized by the British in 1844, I had received an education which ultimately left me and the minds of millions of Africans totally confused as to who we are—Africans or carbon copies of Europeans. This type of education ignores the fact that an African has his own soul and personality, his own traditions and values. In any educational plan all these should be taken into consideration starting at the first grade.

An African child is taught that the ways of his people are primitive, and that if he is to be accepted into a Western oriented and dominated society, he should begin to copy the ways of the White man. Since the African child cannot publicly criticize his parents or even answer back unless he wants the whole neighborhood to rebuke him sharply, he takes his unhappiness and his criticisms of his parents to his friends.

An African child learns from his teachers that the libation that his parents and other members of his extended family pour to the gods and ancestral spirits in times of thanksgiving and need are all paganistic. When my mother came to see me in Accra before my departure for the U.S., she took a glass, filled it with brandy, and pouring the libation, called on my father's ghost, ancestral spirits and the gods to provide me protection while I was away from her. She also asked them to grant me wisdom and guidance in my work. I almost stopped her—not because the ceremony had become so emotional for both of us. I could not reconcile my mother, as a practicing Methodist, going back to the old ways which I had been taught to help uproot from our society.

Our education systematically conditions our minds to the view that the White man has superior brains and talent and that no matter how hard we try we could not accomplish what Europeans have accomplished. They are next to God in omnipotence. Once this idea has been established in our minds, we accept without questioning that our people's ways are primitive. They do not make any progress. There is the need, we conclude, to depart from the old ways.

We are converted to Christianity. We verbally chastise those friends of ours who still worship wooden gods, consult oracles, pour libations publicly, and insist that evil spirits are just a figment of the African imagination. In Catholic and Anglican churches, those of us who have been converted to Christianity kneel before statues, pray, and ask for the same favors that our "pagan" friends are asking from wooden statues passed on to them by our ancestors. We display a lack of an inquiring mind when we do not ask why the one form of worship constitutes idolatry and the other does not. We credit any favors granted to the saints and not to our own gods because our minds are now turned that way.

Until the beatification and canonization recently of the twenty-six Ugandan martyrs, all the saints and angels together with God himself, the Blessed Virgin Mary and Jesus, were all represented to us as White. The only sanctified Black person that an African could identify with was Martin—and he was only "Blessed Martin," one rung below a saint.

Any European, American or British Christian can find in his family tree a saint's name, or at least a name which has some semblance to that of a saint. The decision to give a child a name at his baptism, therefore, presents no problem. The African Christian, especially the Catholic, is confronted by a parish priest who does not see anything Christian about an indigenous African name. After my parents had decided on Kwesi, to indicate I was born on a Sunday, they also had to find me "a good Christian name." So in Africa we have a situation where most people have first a Western Christian name, secondly an African name, and then finally a family name.

I still recall the day that the spiritual director of the Catholic high school I had gone to almost recommended my suspension from school because I had used the name "Kwesi Hayford" on my Easter Communion card instead of Fred. In the U.S., I had a difficult task of explaining to both Black and White Americans why I had a typical English name.

The African's lack of confidence in his ability to achieve what the White man has achieved is epitomized in a saying by the Fanti tribe of Ghana to which I belong. They say "Buronyi ara nye John." In the colonial era, the name John was synonymous with the colonial master. The early Fantis were so deeply taken in by the achievements of the White man's civilization that they had to ask whether or not such accomplishments are within the attainment of a Black man. They had been so systematically brainwashed that they came to the conclusion that "only John" (meaning the White man) "can do all."

There was also the incident involving my own mother, a friend of hers and the friend's daughter. Our entire neighborhood in Elmina was discussing how insolent the daughter was to both young and old. She threw tantrums at the slightest provocation. Her own parents could not control her. I was sitting with my mother in the yard one evening when the mother came to visit. In the course of their conversation, she brought up the subject of her daughter whereupon my mother told her that there was the likelihood that the girl was possessed by some evil spirits. My mother suggested that she should take the daughter to see a fetish priest who could free the girl of the spirits.

She agreed to the suggestion. The question, however, was how did the wife of the Headmaster of a parochial school in a little town like Elmina consult a fetish priest without causing scandal. She suspected that the daughter was abnormal, that she was being troubled by evil spirits. She also knew that under our customs the only way to relieve the girl of the spirits was to let her undergo a certain ritual. But what would be the Church's reaction if it received the information that this is what she had done?

I was unhappy over my mother's suggestion. She still, I thought, could not tear herself away from the old traditions and beliefs. All these years of Methodism had not changed her entirely. Instead of asking her friend to exercise better control of her daughter she was being superstitious. With that frame of mind one can understand the great disappointment I felt when I came to learn that a book dealing with exorcism in America had become one of the country's best sellers. I was even more confused when I learned that a priest had been involved in the exorcism. What are we Africans converting to the Christian faith for if the very things that the White man's religion has been asking us all these years to abandon are now being hailed by the White man?

Before my departure from Ghana, I could not see a Ghanaian woman entering a church in slacks, let alone going to receive Holy Communion in them. The chances are that she would get the message of disapproval from the looks on the faces of other members of the congregation. If she failed to get the message someone would make it a point to let her know. The Catholic priesthood has always been predominantly White in Ghana—Americans (in the Eastern part), Canadians (in the North), Dutch (in the West, and Central Volta Regions). They have built into our minds what is expected to be worn into church. Slacks are excluded. Yet in America women wear them without any sense of guilt.

Many women attend churches in America with their heads uncovered. If these things are part of the Church's new liberal attitude on dress, then the rules should be applied universally. No Ghanaian woman could do that and get away without a reprimand.

People in America walk into churches while the priest is giving his sermon. In Ghana, if you were not physically barred by the marshals, you found that the entrance to the church at the time of the sermon had been barricaded by a velvet rope or two huge sticks crossed together.

It shocked me to see Americans leave the church as they pleased in the middle of the mass. The impression I had was that they had had enough of whatever was being said or done.

Up till today the Church still refuses to grant recognition to the centuries-old Ghanaian marriages under which a young man performs certain laid-down customs after the young lady's parents have agreed to the marriage. This customary marriage could be an expensive affair, a drain on the young man's savings. Yet because the Church does not recognize it, he incurs additional expense in "legalizing" it before the priests. In a country where wedding receptions, gowns and costs are all borne by the bridegroom one can see what this burden can be. Catholics who refuse to take this additional burden are told by the Church that they cannot receive Holy Communion because as far as the Church is concerned they are living in sin. Every country has its own marriage laws. I think it is most unfair to destroy the traditions of a people by imposing too heavily on them something that does not really change their lives. The Catholic Church should come out with a clear line of distinction between laws instituted by Christ which deal with human beings and ecclesiastic laws laid down by the Church, most of which I found unrealistic.

+ + +

In December 1969, I boarded a Greek vessel on a cruise to San Juan, Puerto Rico, St. Thomas, The Virgin Islands, and Aruba and Curacao, Netherlands Antilles. The boat took off from New York Harbor on the feast of the Immaculate Conception, December 8. Oddly enough, this very worldly cruise led to my questioning some of my views on religion.

What first caught my eye when I entered my cabin was a notice asking all passengers to report to the maitre d' for the allocation of tables. I did not think the exercise was called for. Couldn't the management have done this it self without inconveniencing us all? I did report and was given a numbered pink card.

At seven-thirty, fifteen minutes after the gong had been sounded for dinner, I was still in my cabin trying to figure out whether my navy blue bell-bottom pants, white turtle neck shirt, and blue and white Apache scarf and navy blue blazer would meet the approval of the maitre d'.

At a quarter to eight that evening, I finally convinced myself that my outfit was good enough for the dining room. The minute I made my appearance, I noticed that all eyes were on me. This made me extremely uncomfortable, but then it was the first day of sailing. Everyone was on the alert to see if there was someone he knew. There was no better place than the dining room for seeing all the other passengers.

I turned in all directions, searching for my table. All the passengers seemed to be Whites. After a long search through the enormous dining room, I came upon the table. It was located in the extreme right corner of the room. Around it were four beautiful, elegantly-attired Black women. No Whites.

I was astonished. Whose brilliant idea was this that the only five Blacks in a passenger population of four hundred should be singled out and assigned to one table? Now I understood why the maitre d' had insisted on an identification parade.

More doubts began to creep into my mind as to whether Whites were sincere when they talked about integration, and also whether integration would really lead to harmonious race relations.

In my way of thinking, the longer you segregate any group of people on grounds of color, race or sex, the more bitter and hostile you force that group to become toward you. No one can make me believe that America, after all these years, cannot learn this elementary rule.

My attitude towards the White passengers changed at once. Although it was not within me to go out of my way to be unfriendly, I refused to be bothered with the White passengers. If they tried to talk to me, I ignored them. I never laughed at any of their jokes. I stuck to the Black women. All of them were older and not quite as militant as I felt. They were all professional women. One was a business executive. They had come on the boat with well-furnished wardrobes. Nothing made me as proud as escorting these elegantly dressed women into the dining room or to any of the numerous social affairs which were part of the cruise.

It was a question of "Anything you can do I can do better." To my amazement, many of the White passengers either openly or quietly admired our clothes and our dancing at the Captain's fabulous affair and similar events. Each time we appeared in the doorway of any of the evening affairs, I heard complimentary "Aahs," which made me feel six inches taller.

One afternoon I was sitting on the deck with Elsie, one of the Black passengers, when two French Canadian passengers dragged their deck chairs to join us. Another youth, apparently encouraged by the presence of the French Canadians, joined us.

"Say, talk about discrimination, I'd like to know who is discriminating against whom on this boat. It's no longer Whites against Blacks, but Blacks against Whites," the youth said. "I mean, I know you folks all knew each other before you came on board, but at least socialize a little bit."

"I never met any of these people before," Elsie told him.

"What!" the youth exclaimed, "You've got to be joking. You mean you all just met on the boat, and you've been behaving like one great, big, happy family."

"You don't understand," one of the French Canadians intruded. "They have all been sitting at the same table because the maitre d' thought they would be happier with that kind of arrangement."

"Who said that?" I asked hotly.

"The maitre d'. You know, I didn't like you all being put together like that. I asked him about it," the French Canadian replied.

In Aruba the four of us accompanied the other passengers on a night club tour. News had reached us that a Black singer, Leon Bibb, was singing at one of the clubs. Phyjenia, who knew Mr. Bibb personally, said we should all go to cheer him up. We did.

After Bibb's singing, a trio from Venezuela went from table to table to serenade the guests.

"Hey, Phy," I said, "when they get here, I am going to request 'Guantanamara'."

"You'll be lucky if they stop at our table," Phy said.

"Come on, Phy, this is Aruba not America. Besides the trio is Venezuelan."

But if Phy had put a bet on that she could have won some dollars from me. The trio just walked past us to the other table. An exasperated Black waiter whose eyes were evidently missing nothing, marched towards them. An argument ensued. A couple of minutes later the trio made its way toward us. We left before they could reach us.

In the casino, where we took refuge, I had a rude shock. I had not wanted to go there for fear that it was not the right place for a Catholic, but the first person I saw when we entered was the priest who had been saying mass on the boat every morning. He was busy at the roulette wheel.

On my return to Washington I told Bill, a Black friend of mine, about these experiences on the boat. Throughout my narration, Bill sat quietly and looked at me thoughtfully. After he had listened to me, he jumped to his feet. "Put on your coat, Fred. I'm taking you to see a lawyer. I want you to bring a legal action against the shipping company on the grounds of discrimination."

"Bill," I shouted, "you've got to be joking."

"Listen, man, I am just sick and tired of people like you who see discrimination and won't do a thing about it.

You can't fight against a system with your hands folded in your lap."

"Bill, just forget it. One of these days God will take care of all these problems."

"The hell He will," Bill interrupted. "If there is a God, didn't He promise those of you who believe in Him that He will help those who help themselves? I'm tired, Nigger, tired of you religious Black folks and all this crap about God. The White man brought you religion in Africa and he colonized you. He brought my ancestors here in slavery and in all their misery and grief he gave them religion."

I wanted to shut my ears to what he was saying.

"Bill, for the love of God!"

"Fred, for the love of *man,* let's deal in practicalities. If there is one group of people who have been fooled and weakened by religion it is Black people! All because the so-called sacred scriptures contain a lot of junk to appease your mind: 'Blessed are they that mourn for they shall be comforted,' 'Blessed are the poor in spirit for theirs is the kingdom of God,' 'Love them that persecute you,' 'Come unto me all ye that labor,' and after Black folks have listened to that crap, they jump and holler 'Bless the Lord! Alleluia'. That's jive, man. Bull jive—that's what it is."

"You've said too much," I told him.

"Baby," Bill said, "I am not through with you. You're trying to hush me up because I am telling you the truth and it hurts you to hear the truth. Go to any Black neighborhood. Slummy as it may be you always find one building looking prosperous: the church—built with the sweat and labor of the poor people who give towards these buildings and their maintenance even though they can ill-afford it. What do they *get* from the Church? The church's got to be relevant, Fred. It's got to realize that its best followers are the poor. Tell me, what do these poor people get out of being Christians? Name one thing."

"Spiritual welfare," I ventured. Bill laughed.

"Do you really believe that you and the others who go to church every Sunday are more spiritually healthy than those of us who don't? Even in the Soviet Union where religion is not officially recognized, people still differentiate between right and wrong, man. It's in your heart! Your action, treating people like human beings, is what is important. The church has got to make the poor, the Blacks, feel that it can do something for them—not just pray. It should stop building all these huge churches and invest the money in the communities."

In a minute he was gone. We hadn't sued anybody, but my own world was shaken up. In my solitude, Bill's words came rushing back into my mind. The conversation may not have been to my liking, but there was a great deal of truth in what he said. I thought of my own travels through the southern states— North and South Carolina, Georgia, Alabama, Louisiana, Texas, Missisippi. I wanted so much to see these states in their entirety that I had risked traveling through on smaller state roads rather than highways. What had impressed me about these states was the number of churches. Nowhere had I seen as many religious signs posted on the sides of the highways as I did in South Carolina.

In Georgia, Mississippi and Alabama, the story was always the same—Church of Christ, Southern Baptist and United Methodist. As you enter Louisiana and Texas, you see more and more Catholic and Presbyterian churches. Every one of those churches, God knows, is filled to capacity by White church-goers every Sunday. For hours, they sing hymns of praise and listen to the greatest message of God—love. On leaving the churches they become "hearers-of-the-word, not doers." This, to me, makes mockery of God and His words.

In narrating these experiences, I do not overlook the fact that Blacks are sometimes unnecessarily sensitive. There have been cases where discrimination has been charged, but where discrimination was never intended. This is because the racial situation has reached such proportions that there is bound to be mistrust and misunderstanding until people learn to change their attitudes.

There was, for instance, a Washington bus driver on my route to the office. If I ever met one man who was evil, that old White bus driver was. His treatment of his passengers was not dictated by color. He was rude and cold to everyone. He picked up his predominantly White passengers in the area around Wisconsin Avenue and Tilden. At Adams Mill Road onwards, his predominantly Black passengers began to board. I knew that each Black passenger who walked into that bus mistook that evil man for a Negrophobe, not knowing he seemed to hate every-one equally.

I personally would never board any bus and take a seat next to a White person unless I was satisfied that that seat was the only one available. In that case, I would take it, because since both of us paid the same fare I had as much right to a seat as he did. I can hear my friend Hank, whose contention is that to say "Black is beautiful" is to practice racism, accusing me of racist behavior because I avoided Whites. I was not being racist. I was just fed up with being humiliated all the time.

I have seen too many Whites vacate their seats im-mediately when a Black sat next to them on the bus. The possibility exists that had the seat been taken by a White person, the other occupant would have left, anyway. America is one country where people seek solitude so much that it would not surprise me if one sought it on a strange place like a public bus. A White person can take this sort of behavior. To a Black person it seems like just one more humiliation.

I find it hard to believe that in a city the size of Aus-tin, Texas, in the first five hotels and motels where I tried to get a room, I was politely told, "Sorry, but we are full." At the fifth motel on Airport Boulevard, the desk officer, a White woman, told me again what I already knew was coming. I was so angry I could not help my outburst: "Lord! When I get back I sure will have a lot to say. I didn't know that all of Austin could be so hostile as to refuse a Black person a place to lay his head."

The reaction was immediate. The woman jumped from her chair: "I don't think it's color at all. You don't hear too much of that in this city. As a matter of fact, we had a Negro staying here just the other day."

"Madam," I said, as she turned page after page of her register trying to find me a vacant room, "How long have you been in business?"

"Ten years."

"Halleluja! And you're proud to announce you had one Negro staying here the other day."

At that point, the Mexican cab driver who had driven me from hotel to motel and from motel to hotel, could not take any more.

"Come on, let's try some other place," he said.

In the cab, he used the intercom in his car to call his office to make a reservation for me at another motel on the Inter-Regional Highway. Five minutes later, a voice came back on the intercom to say that the reservation had been made and confirmed. It would cost me nine dollars and fifty cents a night.

When I walked into the lobby of the hotel, the story was different. The desk officer, again a woman, denied there had been a reservation.

"But, Madam, you haven't even asked me for my name."

"It's unnecessary."

"Madam, I have a reservation here. You give me a room or there's going to be a whole lot of trouble."

"Are you threatening me?"

"Call it a threat if you like. Bring down the whole of Austin and I'll repeat it."

She picked up some forms and threw them at me with the words "You can sign that."

Who knows—the hotels and motels in Austin all may have been fully booked.

But I did not expect to have equally unsettling experiences at home, after I chose a quiet, respectable apartment, suitable for a young diplomat. I couldn't have been more wrong.

3

Behold, How Good and Pleasant It Is For Brethren To Dwell Together In Unity

(Biblical Expression)

"Green Gables," which I will call the place where I lived in Washington, is a beautiful apartment complex. It had uniformed doormen, a roof-top sun deck fitted with a bar, and secretarial service. Each of its seven hallways had plush, deep red carpeting. Indeed, if you were looking for peace and quiet, you were in the right church and in the right pew. Of its total population only one percent was Black. To be more precise, only six of its ninety apartments and efficiencies were occupied by Blacks: four retired American families, a young lady from the Ivory Coast and myself.

The small percentage of Blacks was not due to discrimination. In the struggle for racial equality and justice, one gain which Blacks have made is a federal law prohibiting the refusal of sale or rental of houses and apartments to people on the grounds of color. There have been charges that even in Washington where the population is seventy percent Black, the law is frequently violated. I obtained apartment 302 of Green Gables with ease. I would say that what made it almost impossible for Blacks to live in Green Gables or any of the deluxe apartment complexes in that neighborhood was the rent, which I thought was prohibitive. A Black friend of mine puts it this way: "You must be high on the hog to be able to live this way."

On two different occasions, Black taxi drivers who drove me to the building wanted to know whether I worked there.

Not long after I moved into Green Gables, strange things began to happen to the elevator service. Old and middle-aged women, who formed the bulk of the residents, appeared frightened at the sight of me. If on my way to the lobby the elevator stopped at another floor, the persons waiting to board the elevator often took one look at me and retreated. If they came in, they had to say something like "My God! You scared me." On my way up to my apartment if I saw other residents coming I pressed the "Open" button to keep the car waiting. Many times they stood outside it and waited for the other elevator.

If someone else entered the elevator first and saw me coming, he just pushed his floor button and left without me. On two occasions when I tried to push my way into the car because the receptionist had told me there was someone waiting to speak to me on my telephone, the elevator doors came shut heavily on my shoulders. They ached for a while.

But if these incidents worried me, I was soon to discover that the worst was yet to come. Some of the residents who saw me in the hallway or at the laundry greeted me with "You must be the new janitor." Once when I picked up my *New York Times* from the lobby, one of the residents said: "Oh, are you the paper boy? I didn't get my paper yesterday." One other resident, entering the building, saw me sitting in the lobby. The doorman was missing, so he assumed that I was the doorman. He turned to me and said: "Boy, we pay you to stand here and open doors, not to sit down there."

I once committed an unpardonable sin—walking bare-chested from my apartment to the refuse chute, a distance of about twenty steps. To the best of my knowledge, there was not a soul in the hallway. On my return to the apartment, the duty desk officer, a friendly Black woman, called me on the house phone:

"Hey, lover boy, you should be ashamed of yourself, advertising yourself in front of all those old women."

"What are you talking about, Myrtle?"

"Oh, you know what I'm talking about. I've had two complaints from your neighbors. You know what they said: 'What are you bringing into this building now?' I asked them what, and they told me about you walking through the halls naked."

I hadn't known that there were Peeping Toms in the building. All these attitudes and comments, I thought, were humiliating. People made the drastic assumption that a young Black person in that building could not possibly be above the level of a janitor or delivery man. It was also at this time that I found out I had an insufferable neighbor.

Mine was not what anyone could describe as a swinging bachelor apartment. Living in a city where people are as clannish as Washington, I had failed to make many friends. The few I had were all married people who did not have the time to do half as much visiting as I would have liked. Occasionally, I had some people in for dinner. My day consisted of work at the Embassy from nine to five-thirty, a combination of supper and the NBC nightly news from six-thirty to seven, and music from seven to nine. By nine o'clock I could hardly keep my eyes open. I warned my friends I would not accept any telephone calls after nine unless it was very urgent.

It was one completely drab life, but when you are foreign in any big American city, you could not ask for much more.

The first time I heard violent knocks on my wall, I was dumb enough to assume that my neighbor was hanging a picture on her own wall. Two Ghanaian friends of mine and their wives were visiting me from New York. All we did was sit and talk. At ten-thirty in the morning, the pounding was first heard. I paid no attention to it. My neighbor was hanging a picture; I had to tolerate a little noise. Soon the house phone rang. The desk officer informed me that my neighbor was bitterly complaining of drumming and dancing going on in my apartment.

I could not believe this. If there had been any drumming and dancing, the first persons to lodge a complaint would be the Black family who lived in the apartment below me. My tenancy agreement had advised that floors should be eighty percent carpeted, but I liked the parquet floor so much that I could not bear to see all of it covered with carpet. Only forty percent of my living and dining space had been covered with rugs. In the event of any disturbance of that nature, the first complaint would most likely come from the family below.

My tenancy agreement also clearly stipulated that after eleven o'clock each night, I was not allowed to be a nuisance to the other tenants by playing music loudly, through the use of my garbage disposal or any other means. But to have a neighbor pounding on walls at ten-thirty in the morning was preposterous!

I told the manager this, hoping that she would carry the message. She did not. My neighbor continued with this rude behavior each time she heard voices in my apartment. This was easy; the walls were no walls at all—they were paper thin. I could hear the neighbor each time she picked up her telephone.

Before I took the apartment I had explained to the manager that in view of my position as Second Secretary for Information in an Embassy, I might be called upon to entertain. I had impressed upon her that I did not want any situation to develop whereby the neighbors would consider me a nuisance. But now my walls were being pounded each time I used my garbage disposal, played music, or had Africans visiting.

Unlike Westerners, Africans (and I was to find out American Blacks, too) relax when we talk. In view of what had been happening, any time my Ghanaian friends visited I became a nervous wreck. How do you explain to your friends that they cannot talk above a whisper?

When I drew the attention of the manager to my problem her advice was that if I planned a party which would go into the early hours of the morning, I should warn her in advance. That way she could explain to any tenant who might call to complain. My walls were being pounded any time of day, my guests were being embarrassed, and there was the manager talking irrelevantly of early hours of the morning.

Long before my problems with my heavy-fisted neighbor, I had become aware that the people who lived on the floor above me were quite incompatible. There was hardly a day that the couple, whoever they were, did not fight. If you were in my kitchen when they got into an argument, you heard every single word. The woman's greatest passion seemed to be calling her husband vile names. After he had had enough of it, he pounced on her. In the midst of the beatings that woman screamed and yelled, and still recovered her breath to call him some more names. The fights usually broke out around midnight. On Saturday, I had to close my ears to the noise.

One afternoon, I was sitting in the lobby waiting for a

friend to pick me up when old Mrs. Mays arrived to relieve the morning desk officer. Mrs. Mays, a grandmother from North Carolina, carried gossip from one resident to another. She knew everything about the residents. She could never quite get used to the fact that I was a tenant and not an employee in the building.

Several of my friends had told me that they did not like to call my number during her shift. She was rude to callers, they said, and often times refused to take messages. She even had the nerve to tell one Ghanaian boy who had insisted on her taking a message, "If I can understand your English I will."

"Mrs. Mays," I said, after she had hung up her coat and hat, "Just as a matter of interest, who are the people in 402?"

She thought it over for a while.

"Oh them," and she damned them with a gesture of her hand. "If you're thinking of complaining about their carrying on, save your breath, Mr. Hayford."

"Why?"

"Because we have already had several complaints from her neighbors—the young lady from Africa and the one from Costa Rica—but the manager won't do a thing about it."

"Why?" I persisted.

"Well, both she and her husband drink a lot. She stays home all day. Her husband goes to work. By the time he gets home, she's all ready to pick on him."

"That's their business. But my business is what is the

management doing about this? I am tired of their late, late shows."

"Nothing. She and the manager are great friends."

"You tell the manager with my compliments then, that if my neighbor calls her again to complain about me, she should not bother me about it. We all pay the same rent and I don't see why some should be treated differently."

Soon after this, I met my wall-pounding neighbor in person for the first time. She had evidently seen me many times.

"I didn't know you were from Africa," the old woman said to me. "For God's sake go to a barber and have a haircut. I don't want you looking like one of these hoodlums in our streets."

She had thought all along that the young man who lived next door to her was an American Black. I thought that perhaps some sort of entente had been established, but I had been so aggravated by her attitude that I looked into the possibility of moving from that apartment into another one within the same building. This was when I learned that "the leopard cannot change its spots."

I had begun to get to know the young lady from the Ivory Coast rather well. I told her about some of the problems I had had with the old lady next door and the couple above me. The couple were her immediate neighbors. She confirmed that she had made many complaints to the manager about the drunks, but nothing had been done. To avoid being awakened late at night, she had abandoned her own bedroom which was next to the drunks, and had taken refuge on her living room sofa.

Her biggest problem, however, was the woman on the other side. She had made no bones about the fact that if she knew there were Blacks in the building she would not for the whole world have moved in. She had first asked the manager for another apartment. When the manager told her she would not move her, she took her case to the property owners.

She was able to build some support from some of the tenants who were not well disposed to having Blacks "invade" the building. But the property owners, from letters later shown to me, told the committee of concerned residents to move out if they did not like having Blacks there. Still this woman did not intend to give up. She harrassed the young lady from the Ivory Coast anytime she heard voices, anytime she heard music. She even screwed up enough courage one day to knock on the door of the Ivorrien lady and tell her to her face, "Why don't you move to where you belong?"

I can put up with a lot. Amelie, the Ivorrien, cannot. She made that woman take to her heels. After there were no more complaints even though Amelie went to extremes—her television set, radio, tape recorder and record player were all on simultaneously.

Amelie and I walked into the building one afternoon to find one of the desk officers, a White lady, hollering at the young Black man who opens doors. Both of us were friendly with the doorman. We asked what had happened.

According to the desk officer, one of the residents had come in with two bags of groceries. The weight was more than she could carry so she left one of the bags at the desk and instructed that the doorman should bring it up. The desk officer was upset because after thirty minutes had elapsed the doorman was still nowhere to be found.

I looked at Amelie. She looked at me. Since when had residents been accorded that privilege, we both wanted to know. We could recall many times when we had been called to go down to collect deliveries left at the desk. Double standards, evidently, existed in the management of the building.

Of the four American Black families in the building, Jim Carter was the youngest. He and his White wife lived in one of the three absurdly-priced penthouses. Mr. Carter was a man I could not help liking, but except for his smile, he never seemed to have anything to say or do with any of the tenants, Black or White. I did not like Mrs. Carter. Each time I saw her in the lobby she had been complaining of discriminatory practices in the building.

It was on record that the Black tenants seldom complained. So I did not see how Mrs. Carter, whose only link with us, after all, was the fact that she was married to a Black man, could see all those discriminatory practices against her every day. Besides, she had a traveling job and was gone most of the time. Her husband moved to upstate New York to take a new job. The only time that the two of them lived in the apartment was on weekends.

Just as I entered the building one afternoon, the desk officer on duty called me to ask if I would oblige her with a favor. The woman who lived in the apartment below the Carters was constantly complaining about running water from the Carter apartment. The gurgling was twenty hours a day, and was driving her insane. Would I, she asked me, be kind enough to go with her and the other woman to check the taps in the Carter apartment?

Under normal circumstances, I would flatly have refused. On that occasion I agreed. We let ourselves into the apartment with the extra key that the management keeps for emergencies. Every tap in that apartment was closed. The neighbor was shamefaced, but she still swore she had heard the water running all the time. Possibly Jim Carter's ancestral spirits inhabited the apartment in his absence.

+ + +

Of the American cities that I had the privilege to visit, these took my heart completely—Los Angeles, San Francisco, Atlanta, Denver, Houston, Raleigh and Winston-Salem, New Orleans, and Columbia, South Carolina. In all these cities, there was little or no evidence of decay and filth. There was plentiful greenery and signs of prosperity.

But none of them, I daresay, could equal my "native" Washington. Around spring when the trees and flowers begin to bloom, the District of Columbia is one large garden. One of my favorite pastimes in spring, summer and fall was to ride the buses or drive my own car through certain parts of Rock Creek Park, where the view was magnificent. It used to break my heart when the bus reached 16th Street and Irving and I had to disembark and walk to the office.

Anyone who is familiar with the area around Porter Street and Adams Mill knows what a glorious view it is. In front of me in the bus one morning were two White ladies. As the bus made its way through the neighborhood, one suddenly remarked to her friend.

"Oh look at those roses and hydrangeas; what a beautiful neighborhood."

"I hope this neighborhood doesn't go down any more. It used to be so much better than this until they moved in and drew the people here away," the other one remarked.

What she was referring to was pretty obvious. The neighborhood was now full of working-class Blacks and a few young Whites. A federal law prohibiting discrimination in housing had made it possible for Blacks to buy and rent homes in the area, once a solid-White neighborhood.

Even though the Blacks had taken over from Whites who had fled to the suburbs, there was evidence that they worked their fingers to the bone to maintain the neighborhood as beautifully as any suburb I had seen. In the view of our friend, however, the neighborhood had gone down because Blacks had moved in. To millions of such prejudiced Whites all Blacks are the same—they must be kept at a distance.

A Black man could be a professional. He could have been educated in Ivy League schools and hold a job that pays more than most White men make, but the minute he buys or rents a home in an all-White neighborhood, there is a general upset. A stampede begins. Whites begin to sell their homes and move out into the suburbs.

Now that the Blacks seem to be following the Whites everywhere, I wonder where the Whites will be moving out to next? Still, I found areas of suburbs that seemed the prerogative of Whites and others that seemed to have been apportioned only to the Black middle class. I ate dinners in lovely homes in the suburbs where some of my friends explained it would be almost impossible for even wealthy Blacks to move in. Even if they could afford the cost of homes, the residents were so closely-knit that they would prevent the sale of homes in certain neighborhoods to Blacks.

With exception of Atlanta, Durham, Washington's Blagden Avenue, Petersburg (Virginia) and Greensboro (North Carolina), most of the homes occupied by Blacks in America are what one might choose to call "hand-me-downs." When one Black man buys a home in a White neighborhood and frightens the Whites into flight, the Blacks take over. Then the once all-White neighborhood becomes a rich ghetto.

It is still debatable whether the costs of these "hand-me-down" homes are not prohibitive. The number of Blacks who can afford new homes is very, very small.

The flight of Whites to the suburbs is one subject that I freely discussed with some White acquaintances who prided themselves on not having anything against Blacks, but had still moved away from the cities. Almost all of them attributed their movement to one or two of three reasons: (1) Lack of good schools in the cities; (2) a crime wave in the cities; (3) pollution in the cities. I had to laugh at these, because from my little knowledge of Americans these arguments sounded like excuses, for this reason— one of the American institutions I found remarkable and worthy of emulation was the capacity and the ability of its people to fight and lobby against anything they do not want. They write to their congressmen, they mount a leaflet campaign on pavements and from door to door. They bring in the press, the television and the radio. What I am trying to say is if Whites were genuinely concerned about bad schools, crime and the quality of environment in the cities, they would have used the powerful weapons they have to change the situation, instead of throwing up their hands and leaving.

Millions of Whites have fled because they just cannot see themselves living next door to a Black man. Some of my White acquaintances tried to make me believe they had nothing against Blacks. I saw through most of them. So long as a Black person could keep his distance, he was acceptable. So long as a Black man stayed away from places he was not wanted, he was liked.

Some of the prejudices against Blacks were simply incredible.

I stayed one week with a well-to-do family in a small city on the East Coast. In their neighborhood, one seldom saw a Black face. If you did see one it was that of a domestic helper in a white uniform. I had that privilege of being a guest because of my friendship with the son of my hosts, whose ideas and associations with Blacks had finally forced him into self-imposed exile in Africa.

While in college in the U.S., Eric had always brought home some of his Black friends to stay for a weekend or more. This dismayed the neighbors. His parents, who were extremely wealthy and of independent minds, made no effort to stop their son from bringing in any more Blacks. If anything, they encouraged it and thus won the reputation of being "Nigger lovers."

While I was there, someone broke into the Johnson's house. Mr. Johnson had gone to work at the time of the robbery, and Mrs. Johnson was showing me the city. Whoever was responsible had it easy because the Johnsons never locked any door. Except for a purse containing sixty dollars, nothing was taken. The matter was reported to the police. I was walking on the pavement the next day when I saw two women talking to each other. If they were not already discussing the theft, they started when they saw me. One said very loudly: "Well, what else do they expect with all those Niggers coming in and out of that house. This neighborhood has never known anything like that."

We are told, and I admit it with some reservations, that each time Blacks move into a neighborhood the value of property is depreciated. I say with reservations, because to begin with that statement is a sweeping generalization. There are many, many Black neighborhoods in America where the value of property went up at the time the Blacks were ready to move in. If it is the general unsanitary conditions of the inner cities that make some Whites come to that conclusion, then all I can say is that filth, crime, prostitution, and alcoholism are not peculiar to America's Black ghettos. They are the general condition in any part of any country where there is a concentration of poor people.

A typical example is South Philadelphia. Some portions are just as bad if not worse than some Black ghettos. I raised this once in conversation. My information was that many of the residents were poor Greeks and Italians. Poverty and degradation are no particular color.

I maintain that it is nothing other than old prejudices that makes it impossible for Whites to accept us into their neighborhoods.

But give the devil his due. At least in Washington, a foreign land, I was able to walk freely through White neighborhoods. The residents may not have appreciated it; they showed it by acting nervous no matter how well I was dressed. But it could have been worse, as I well knew. Before independence came to the Ghanaians, "bungalows" as they were referred to, were lily-White areas. During mango season Ghanaian kids would sneak into the bungalows to pick up the friuts—which the British had no use for, but which we loved. The occupants of the bungalows knew the kids were there only for the mangoes which had fallen from the trees and were left to rot, and yet they unleashed their dogs on us. And the land on which this happened was ours. To this day I, like many Ghanaians, have not overcome my fear of dogs.

I cannot accept the theory that the problem of the Black man in America is simply that of the minority. It is not. It is based on the stereotyped view of Whites that Black men were created to be "hewers of wood and carriers of water." Whites the world over maintain that the Black man was born in servitude to Whites and that both in intellect and in all human endeavors a Black man can never be equal to a White.

In addition to this traditional White view of the Black man as a beast of burden, there seems to be another view which is rather distasteful—that of the Black man as a sex object.

The only reason conflicts between the Black and White races have been more pronounced in the U.S., in South Africa and Rhodesia is that there are more Blacks living in these countries. The problem of White against Black exists all over Europe. In Asia, Latin America and even in the Middle East, the Black man is still found at the bottom of the ladder.

African students who study in the East European

countries learn that racism exists even in Communist countries as soon as they started being friendly with the girls from these lands. Sweden, we are told, is a progressive country. What happened recently when the young people there started to demonstrate against U.S. involvement in Southeast Asia? It was no longer "Yankee, go home." It was "Nigger, go home. They need you on the plantation." This epithet referred to the U.S. Ambassador to Sweden, who was Black. It is on record that Sweden is one of the European countries where the Black man is always a great favorite of the ladies.

If Whites don't want to live with Blacks, it must be because of the mental image they have formed of Black people. I became determined to find out just what that image was, and who had foisted it on America.

4

Give A Dog A Bad Name

(Old English Proverb)

"You're putting us on, Mrs. Colbert," the little girl said shortly after the introduction.

"What are you talking about, Margaret?" her teacher asked.

"You told us we were going to have a speaker from Africa," the girl answered.

"Well, right here, young lady. Mr. Hayford is from Africa. I told you he's from the country of Ghana."

"I don't believe it. He looks just like one of us," the girl said.

"Yes. He looks just like one of us," five hundred or so fourth, fifth and sixth graders jammed in the school auditorium shouted together.

I smiled. I had gone through a similar experience in a Catholic high school in an affluent neighborhood in Norfolk, Virginia. The exchange between Margaret and her social science teacher, Mrs. Colbert, had occurred in one of the poorest sections of Southeast Washington. The irony of the exchange was that all the children, the principal and Mrs. Colbert were Black. I had gone to the school at the invitation of the social science teacher to talk to the children about Ghana, and to answer any questions that might arise out of the meeting.

Little Margaret and the other children were bewildered at seeing me. Evidently, they had anticipated a man walking onto that stage wearing a loin cloth, with a spear and shield in his hands and a ring in his nose. This is the twentieth century image of Africa in the U.S. It is an image which exists in the minds of young and old, rich and poor, Black and White. It is an image built by the colonials and perpetuated by the American news media. It has enjoyed considerable success primarily for two reasons: (1) It boosts the ego of prejudiced Whites; (2) psychologically, it has helped in making some Blacks thankful that they are not a part of the jungle people.

I was only ten when I first heard about pen-pals. In my school in Sekondi-Takoradi, practically half of the pupils were writing to someone in England, the U.S., France and Germany. Of the four countries, the U.S. and England were, without doubt, the most popular since there was no language barrier. I found American pen friends in Phoenix, Cedar Rapids, Minneapolis, Boston and New York City. Some of the questions these children asked me in their letters were not only infantile but sometimes close to unbelievable. The most frequent concerned the wild animals which run through the jungles of Africa, our residences which supposedly were in the tops of trees, the poverty and diseases which they supposed were everywhere.

The development of my country had nowhere reached that of the U.S., Britain, Germany or France, we agreed. Notwithstanding, we expected young people from other lands to credit us with some degree of civilization. Surprisingly, we never lost our tempers at any of these questions. If anything, I and my friends who had been asked similar questions laughed at such ignorance. After all, we assumed that the whole object of exchanging letters between two people from two different countries who had never met was to learn from each other. So in my replies, I tried to dispel some of the myths that they believed about Africa.

Very few Africans, I told them, had ever seen a lion, elephant or rhinoceros. I explained that the only harmful creatures that the Ghanaians were familiar with were snakes. I told them what had happened in Elmina the day that an herbalist (popularly known in Western society as a witch doctor) had brought a hyena into the town. Half of the population walked to his house to see the chained animal. For the people of Elmina that was a red-letter day—a day that many of them never saw again.

In 1968, twenty years after my introduction to this exchange of letters and gifts between thousands of Ghanaians and foreigners, I arrived in Washington—to find to my dismay that the myths about Africa are still as strong as they were before. Perhaps if I had not assumed the job of Information Officer, these stereotyped views about Africa and Africans would not have hit me so hard. But in that capacity I had to read extensively to find out what the national and local newspapers were saying about Africa generally and Ghana in particular.

I also had to watch television networks closely to hear what comments were passed on the African political scene. My government was also interested in the image that the networks projected of Africa.

Gradually, I learned that the image of Africa in the U.S. had not undergone any change whatsoever since my school days. The newspapers, journals, and television persisted in projecting Africa the way they wanted it seen. They referred to the people either as "natives" or "primitive tribes." The "Tarzan" series was typical of the programs on Africa. Articles and commentaries told only the bleak aspects of developments in Africa. The impression that is bound to be made on any American reader or listener by these programs and commentaries is that Africa is nowhere near civilization—that it is still a wild continent plagued with disease, poverty, hunger and tribalism.

One would have thought that after slavery and colonialism, the media would at least leave Africans alone if they had nothing complimentary to say or show. I was reminded of the Western films showing uncivilized Indians one sees so often on television—why would the

Americans not leave the Indians alone? Were all these an attempt to relieve the minds of Americans, to show them that the Indians and the Blacks had to undergo what they did because they were uncivilized, rowdy and barbaric? I thought that this picture had already been deeply painted in the minds of the White world. No further proof of it was necessary.

My job provided me with ample opportunity to measure the damage that has been done to Africa as a result of articles and television shows. Since its independence in 1957, Ghana has continued to dominate the political scene in Africa. This has had three noticeable effects: (1) The U.S. newspapers cannot afford to ignore events in Ghana. They can color and twist these events to suit their editorial policies, but the fact still remains that they cannot ignore them. (2) American students majoring in African politics turn their attention to Ghana. They use the embassy as a source of resource material. This is done either in interviews or requests for releases and documents. (3) In their new-found identity with Africa, American Blacks look up to Ghana more than to any other African country.

Before my arrival in the U.S., African ambassadors and diplomats had toured the country, talking to church groups, university students, high school students and women's organizations. The diplomats have mingled with Americans of all levels and all shades of opinion. American tourists, Peace Corps volunteers and State Department officials have returned from Africa and shared their experiences with many. In spite of all the good work that these people have done, I found that the majority of the people I came into daily contact with still associated Africa with the jungles.

Like my predecessors and colleagues in other African missions, I encouraged visits to the embassy and discussions. Students came to us from many parts of the U.S. If they did not come in groups, they came by themselves—students of political science, militants with frightening looks, Black Panthers, church groups and prisoners. When they were not visiting the embassy, I was visiting them. Their questions were often embarrassing and sometimes humiliating. I was gratified, however, by the knowledge that these people admitted they did not have and were desirous of learning.

My audiences would usually refer me to an article which appeared in such and such a journal considered "well informed" on Africa, or to remarks that such and such a professor, "an expert on African affairs," had made. Unfortunately, we live in a world in which everything credited to an expert or anything which appears in a reputable newspaper is accepted as the gospel truth.

Three-quarters of the articles published on Africa by American newspapers and journals give African embassies violent headaches. If the African diplomats, especially those dealing with information, are to survive, they have no alternative but to try to disregard these articles.

I wonder why some foreign correspondents sent to Africa do not check their facts. Their articles on Africa tend to ridicule Africans and their governments. But these correspondents know that, with the exception of Sierra Leone which institutes court actions against irresponsible journalists, the worst that any African government could do is to deport them—an action that African governments resort to unhappily.

The correspondent of one Baltimore paper was deported from Ghana at the time of the First Republic. The deportation order was revoked by the military government which took over from the First Republic. The government's decision to revoke that order may have been necessitated by its desire to improve its relations with the U.S., which had gone sour at the time of the First Republic.

One would have thought that this particular correspondent would show an appreciation of the new government's gesture by being accurate and objective, but his dispatches from Accra still display the same old inaccuracy and bias. Senegal has since declared him *persona non grata*.

After the newspapers comes the worst enemy—television. I went to the office one morning without the slightest idea that a Washington channel had shown a film the night before depicting Africans as savages. For the whole morning, my telephone was kept busy. Every caller was furious. Ghanaians were calling, Black Americans were calling—all to complain about the film. What, the callers demanded, were we African embassies doing to stop such derogatory projections? My ambassador, E. M.

Debrah, and the then-ambassador of Sierra Leone, John Akar, sent a protest note to the manager of the channel. The station barely acknowledged receipt of that letter.

I remember one man who said he had spent ten years in and out of Africa. Before his appearance on network TV, the station gave such wide publicity to the program that I thought "For once, someone will talk about Africa as it really is." I was fooled. His heavily advertised program told the same old story. He told viewers of the jungles of Africa and its lions. He also spent considerable time talking of the "Afro" bush hairdo, which he did not see in Africa.

Then came NBC's "First Tuesday" which featured Liberia. I missed it, but the uproar was the same. Even White Americans wrote or called us to deplore such a one-sided feature.

One of Disneyland's most popular attractions in Anaheim, California, is the so-called "Jungles of the World." Although titled "of the world," half of these jungle scenes are devoted entirely to Africa, and the same old stereotyped image of Africa is recreated in make-believe plastic. Disneyland ventures even further. It depicts not only the jungles, it also shows you the cannibals.

In one corner, elephants charge at a White "Bwana" and his African servants. True to White imagination, the "Bwana" has taken refuge in a palm tree while the struggling khaki-clad African servants wait for him to make room in the tree.

When an African diplomat has become familiar with such racism, he is not very impressed by letters and long-distance telephone calls from television stations and publishers of educational materials, urgently requesting information and photographs for something they are publishing or featuring on Ghana. What I find interesting is that these institutions nearly always insist that photographs should be on the tribes, the villages, farmers and craftsmen—not on modern Africa.

Only two out of ten ever asked for photographs showing Ghana as she really is today—a combination of the ancient and modern. If representatives of these educational publishers came to my office and I gave them a portfolio of photographs on modern Ghana, they made it clear they were disappointed. Slides I forwarded to publishers by mail were very representative, showing all sides of Ghana. I always knew even before the slides left my office which ones would be rejected and which ones accepted for inclusion in the publication. Those on modern Ghana almost always came back to me a week after mailing with a cover letter regretting the inability of the editor to use them.

After these experiences with the news media, I was not so enthusiastic when my ambassador told me that he had agreed to appear on a "Black Journal" program marking the opening of the Journal's office in Addis Ababa, Ethiopia. Had not a telephone call interrupted our conversation, I would have advised him against accepting the invitation. "Black Journal" was devoted to

Blacks but financed by the same White power structure. Was it going to be more objective than the rest or was it going to tell Black viewers about the jungles that they had heard about time and time again?

I returned to my office to find the day's mail waiting on my table. I picked up an envelope marked "Black Journal." The letter inside read: "We, as Africans in America, need to see the positive side of Africa so that we can develop a much-needed psychological identity with Africa to develop our roots of identification. All of our reporting will be of a positive nature. The 'White Press' goes to Africa to seek out sensationalism, and we get the picture of Africa as a Tarzan and Jane land and a constant bed of revolution. This picture we hope to correct. Brown stresses that there is a permanent need for a dialogue between Africans in Africa and Africans in America because of our cultural ties and our political needs."

This sounded interesting. But the question the release did not answer and which Tony Brown, the producer of the show, didn't bring up during our meeting was: Would it serve the interest of the people who are financing this project to give a truthful picture of Africa? Does a cultural and political identity of "Africans in Africa and Africans in America" not pose a threat to someone?

In the midst of all the gross misrepresentations, as a sort of "final straw," the *Washington Daily News* of August 6, 1970 carried the following news item: "Africa Blood and Guts, a Cinematic industries release, opens

August 21 at the Criterion. The film deals with inhuman brutality and terror on the Dark Continent."

Invitations asking Embassy officials either to talk or make appearances at functions were sometimes more than we could cope with. What we tried to do was encourage some of our Ghanaian students to go instead, since from a public relations point of view, the more such invitations we accepted, the more beneficial it was to us. I could not get the students to agree. Dinner invitations were instantly rejected.

They explained that they were sick of being asked more questions than necessary during some of these dinners. Some of the questions, they said further, embarrassed them. As much as I sympathized with the students, I told them that the only way to correct the situation was to expose Americans to ourselves, rather than leaving them at the mercy of the media.

I was concerned over the attitudes of the Ghanaian students. If our students were going to leave for home thinking that Americans made no effort to know or understand Africans, where were we headed? You do not strengthen or improve relations when one side humiliates you and the other side withdraws into himself to avoid any more humiliation.

There was the case of one Ghanaian student who was invited to dinner by an American family. When the dinner was served, Amon found that the steak was very rare. Blood ran out of the steak like a newly slaughtered lamb. The average Ghanaian is upset by even a medium-rare steak. When Amon drew the attention of this to the hostess, one of the guests, a woman, took offense. She insisted that the young man was showing off. From her information, Africans ate raw, uncooked meat. She added, "You should thank your stars that your hostess, on account of our not being used to raw meat, cooked this steak a little."

The argument went on till the young man, unable to take any more, left the house.

If this woman did not know how Africans cook their food, all she had to do was to keep quiet and ask that question politely.

I had a similar encounter the very first day I arrived in the U.S. I had gone to the lobby of the Windsor Park Hotel in Washington, where I was staying, to telephone a few friends. I was used to telephones with figures only, so when I found that the phone in the lobby had both numbers and letters of the alphabet, I was confused. I approached a White woman in the next booth, and asked her politely to explain its operation to me. After she had done so, she turned to me and asked, "Where are you from?"

"Africa," I told her.

"Well, I must warn you, young man, it's not going to be easy for you," she said. "Racial-wise, I mean. You just don't talk to a White lady. That is taking liberties."

In the course of three days in April 1969 my office was deluged with letters from a grade school in a town in New Jersey. The deluge was nothing new to the information section of the embassy. We counted an average of twenty letters a day from grade school pupils who were writing reports on Ghana and wanted the embassy's help.

This number excludes the many received from high school and college students, professors and organizations. But the letters from New Jersey were of particular importance because each one of them had the same story to tell. Their teacher, the writers said, had a sister who lived in Ghana. Their teacher had brought her to school to talk about Ghana. All that these kids, whose minds were being molded, heard about Ghana was about the poverty, diseases and the beggars who go to White people's bungalows for alms. To rub salt into the wound, the teacher asked the children to write to the embassy for photographs showing "the primitive tribes."

Knowing the warmth and the hospitality of Ghanaians, I can imagine that woman telling the Ghanaians how much she and her husband enjoyed the country and the people. Was our only reward what she said to the New Jersey pupils on her return?

This story also recalls to mind the number of tourists who go to Africa and return to produce out of their suitcases their most prized souvenirs—photographs and films showing the worst in Africa. In total disregard for human feelings, they will invite Africans to the screening of these films.

I traveled quite a bit in the U.S. The more I saw of the country, the more irritated I became at the gross misrepresentation of Africa by the news media and some other people. I came to find that poverty, hunger and disease were by no means social evils that one finds only in Africa. They were right there in the U.S. for all to see. In rural Virginia, North and South Carolina, Georgia, Alabama, Mississippi and Louisiana, I saw with my own eyes the kind of shacks that foreign correspondents in Africa had made big stories out of. I saw with my own eyes some of the thick, green forests and swamps which in Africa have been described as primitive jungles.

I could hardly concentrate on my driving as I looked at this other America in total disbelief. The forests around me were too dense to be called anything but jungles. I saw Black women and children returning from cotton and tobacco farms. I had thought that these were all things of the past that I had heard and read about, but not something that I would ever see. These people's living conditions were deplorable.

All I wanted to do at that moment was to vent my spleen on any American—Black or White. To tell him "Look, why don't you people talk more about this?" I wanted someone like another White friend of mine whose theory was that Africans cannot write about Africa for the American mass media because if they did, they could not tell the whole truth.

"Who writes about America for the Africans?" I queried.

"The Americans."

"If the Americans can write about themselves for the Africans, what makes you think that we cannot write about ourselves for you? Every people understand their own situation better than foreigners." That had silenced him.

In Mobile, Alabama, I had the chance at least to say what I felt.

I was driving with Bob, a White friend of mine. We were stopped intermittently by the police. A Black man driving with a White man in a car with northern plates did not seem too satisfactory to the southern police. Bob knew all the tricks. Since we were driving on country roads and were more vulnerable, he cautioned me against speeding. We paid attention to all the road signs. We had our licenses ready for the police wherever they stopped us. My only concern was that I had left home my diplomatic I.D. Ordinarily, I never go anywhere outside Washington without it.

My heart was in my mouth as Bob and I entered the bar behind the Greyhound bus station in Mobile, Alabama. I was afraid that the bartender, a White woman, would refuse to serve me. She did not. People stared. I was nervous. Bob got into an argument with me as to whether I should eat that hamburger I had ordered and which he thought was junk.

Just then I felt a hand on my shoulder. I turned, fearing the police. It was a White woman. "Sir," the lady said, "I hear you have an accent. Where are you from?"

"Ghana," I replied.

"Ghana!" The lady screamed with delight. "What a

small, small world," she added as she bit into her hamburger.

I was becoming more and more uncomfortable in that bar—a Black sitting in a southern bar, making conversation with two Whites who did not appear to be aware of the curious, hostile eyes. I wondered what the people in the bar who looked at us and giggled were saying under their breath.

It turned out that the White lady was on her way from Lake Charles, Louisiana to Birmingham to see her only brother who was going to take a job as an engineer with the Ghanaian government. She invited Bob and me to go with her to Birmingham to see the brother. We politely turned down the invitation.

By the time the story had been told to us I had had two beers. The alcohol was gradually taking effect on me. I was high and relaxed, and my words tumbled out: "You know, after driving through Alabama, I think your brother will feel at home in Ghana."

She missed my sarcasm. I tried again. "Alabama, I am told, is a very poor state, but I am sure that the people are walking on gold without realizing it."

"What do you mean?" our new acquaintance asked.

"I mean that if only the state government would spend a little money developing its dense forests, there will be absolutely no need for Americans to go all the way to Africa on safari. The jungle is right here in Alabama." The woman's smile faded. "Oh, that's too much," she said, raising her hand as if to hit me.

"Hey watch it," I smiled, "You're not in the north, you're in Cracker country. The K.K.K. is going to get you for carrying on in public with a Nigger. By that time I'll be gone."

"The K.K.K. is no longer in existence," the woman said flatly.

"I left Atlanta thirty-six hours ago. The K.K.K. was meeting then at Stone Mountain."

"How do you know? Are you an agent or something?" she asked.

"I just have my eyes and ears open." (I later read in the *Washington Post* that J. Edgar Hoover estimates the strength of the K.K.K. to be 4,300. He thinks, however, that the Black Panthers is the most dangerous organization in the U.S.A.)

"Well, still I won't call Alabama a jungle," the woman said. "These trees you see in Alabama have no snakes hanging on them and you don't have any pygmies running through it with spears and arrows."

"If there were no wild animals in these forests, there wouldn't be any need for posting 'No Hunting' signs all along the stretch," I told the American lady.

As a professional journalist, I could have taken photographs of the jungles of Alabama, the swamps of Louisiana and the rural conditions in the Dixie states. I could have circulated these photos among African newspapers to counter the image of America, based on movies, as a "land of milk and honey."

But if I or any other Ghanaian journalist had dispatched this kind of photo and written observations for any of our newspapers, the first of such a series published would have brought a sharp reaction from the U.S. Embassy in Accra.

The U.S. Embassy would have deemed the article and supporting photos as unfriendly, and would accordingly have lodged an official protest with the Ghanaian government. Fearful that the U.S. might cut its aid to Ghana if the series were continued, my government would have been forced to pressure the papers not to carry such articles. Such is reality.

Long before my arrival in the U.S., one of Ghana's political afternoon papers, the *Evening News,* published an article in which it accused the Australian government of racism with regard to New Guinea. Because that paper was government-owned, the then-Australian ambassador took a copy of the paper, went to the Ministry of Foreign Affairs, and when he was granted an interview by the Principal Secretary, pointed to the article and said in a rage, "This is bullshit."

We can swear too, but the chance for an African diplomat to reach the U.S. State Department with a few African bad words unfortunately has never occurred. The government, we are told, has no control over journals, American newspapers and television. They are all privately owned. So, in the name of democracy, they indulge in what sometimes amounts to irresponsible journalism.

I do not think that any African government owes foreigners an apology for the existence of hunger, disease and poverty. Any foreign paper which wants to make an issue out of these should ask all the former colonial masters—Britain, France, Portugal and Belgium—to give an account of their performances in their former possessions.

Western papers talk constantly of the lack of technical know-how in Africa and how the African nations may have to rely on the West for expert advice in certain sectors for a long time. In case anybody has not learned his history of colonialism in Africa, I wish to place a few facts at his disposal.

My country formally became a British protectorate in 1844. No university was founded there until 1948, after more than a century of British rule. The bulk of Ghanaians who received any education before independence were the products of missionary schools—namely the Catholic, Methodist, Presbyterian and Anglican. There were only twenty high schools for a population of six and a half million persons before independence. Of these, only one, Achimonta, was founded by the British government.

Either through lack of funds or for other reasons, the missionary schools placed so much emphasis on liberal arts that at the time of independence, when many British expatriate officers started to leave because they could not serve under Blacks, there was a dearth of doctors, engineers, architects and all kinds of personnel with technical skills.

Ghana has invested quite a large sum of money in the

training of doctors and the provision of badly needed medical attention for our people. In spite of these human and financial investments, there are still only seventy-five hospitals for a population of eight and a half million. There is one doctor to every 10,700 people. What then did Britain do about the health and education needs of the country it colonized for a hundred and three years?

This situation exists not only in Ghana, but also in Nigeria, Sierra Leone, Gambia, and in the East African nations of Uganda, Kenya, Tanzania and Zambia. Reserves that these nations had at the time of independence are now being spent to provide facilities which should have been provided long, long ago.

I do not say any of this with the intention of making any White person hit his chest and say "Mea culpa, mea maxima culpa." I don't think the majority of the Black world is interested in his guilt or his apologies. We try to forget and forgive colonialism and slavery. But when the people who created these situations speak against us, it is easy to become defensive.

I become angry every time I read or hear somewhere that some brilliant scientist says that the reason Africans and Black Americans have not made enough headway in education is that they suffer from certain genetic deficiencies. Rubbish! The picture was painted by the White man, and he continues to see it as he wants to see it.

5

Hush
Now! Don't
Explain

(Singer Billie Holliday)

The location was in affluent Potomac, Maryland. The living room in which I sat, together with two other African diplomats, sipping cocktails with our host and hostess, was beautifully furnished. None of us had ever met before. I had been in the District of Columbia only five months and was finding it difficult to meet people on a social basis, so when one of Washington's groups which arrange hospitality programs for foreign diplomats asked if I would be interested in being entertained in an American home, I said yes.

The other two newly arrived African diplomats and I had immediately been put in touch with our host and hostess. Our host was watching a football game on television. We had told him that we were not familiar with the game, so every now and then he would explain the game

121

to us. There was a break for commercials. A young Black lady, advertising cigarettes, appeared on the screen.

Our hostess, to our utmost surprise, jumped from her seat, dashed to the box and snapping, "These Niggers are taking over everything," switched the channel to another one. Suddenly she realized what she had done.

"Gentlemen," she said. "You know I am not prejudiced, but I believe in a man working hard for a living. My husband and I have worked very hard for everything we've got, but these Negroes just want something for nothing. They don't like to work. All they want to do is tear this country apart. All you Africans are different. I have met quite a few and I can't help liking you all. Why can't our Negroes be the same?"

I had heard the story before. Both in New York and in Washington if I gave service to people when they came into my office, some would always seize the opportunity to tell me how different Africans are from the American Negroes. What my hostess was saying was nothing new.

By her own admission, later in our conversation, my hostess had never invited into her home any Black American person. The chances of one being invited there were very remote. The only Blacks who were ever found in that house were delivery men and they were admitted through the back door. What I deduced from our conversation that night was that my host and hostess did not know any Black Americans at all.

They never will, with that attitude, so what justification do they have to make comparisons with the Africans whom they occasionally wined and dined?

These invitations from White American families, I was later to discover, have helped to create dissension between the Africans living in or visiting the U.S. and the Black Americans. The Blacks resent the hospitality shown us, and understandably so. If I were a Black American I would be hurt, too, by someone who all along has refused to acknowledge my presence merely because of my color, but who would invite another Black person from another country into his home.

What I do not accept, though, is the feeling among Blacks that these invitations amount to real acceptance of the Africans. After three and a half years in the U.S., I dispute that claim. I think that each case should be treated on its own merit. I have been entertained in homes where I have had no reason to doubt the sincerity of the host and hostess, who saw people as people. They had no pretenses. They just like people. Their friendships were not based on color. But even some of these families admittedly had never invited any Blacks into their homes or had any association with them—not because they were anti-Black.

The racial situation in the U.S. unfortunately has reached a point where Blacks brand every White person as a racist and where Blacks who are friendly with decent-minded Whites are considered as traitors to the cause. This, I think, is rather tragic. I am happy that I am leaving

America with the assurance that not every White American is a racist.

As I saw it some Whites simply have no means of making the acquaintance of Blacks. The races are sadly separated from each other. We have already seen the situation as it exists in housing and churches. There are also the prejudices of parents and neighbors which weigh heavily on some. But once these color-blind Whites have made acquaintances of Blacks, each race teaches the other a thing or two.

Then there are the invitations that I choose to call "window-dressing dinners." Under normal circumstances, some of the hosts and hostesses involved would never be bothered with Africans. They are approached by various government agencies in order to introduce the Africans to American family life or to help the Africans come to believe that America does not practice racism.

At such window-dressing dinners the race question becomes a subject of discussion. Your hosts whitewash themselves. They impress upon you how liberal they themselves are, but how they have had to cut themselves off from the Black cause because of the Black man's inherent limitations. Africans who have just arrived and lack a proper assessment of the situation believe this.

What is more, many of the African students in America are private students who support themselves. They live in or around the inner cities. They are daily witnesses to the evils of poverty-stricken neighborhoods. They judge. They forget entirely that back in their own countries similar conditions exist. They come to the same conclusions about Negroes that American Whites have already made.

I do not exonerate African diplomats. Some make the same mistakes. When they drive through the inner cities the things they see make some of them attribute the plight of the American Black man to his own doing. Perhaps if I had not been trained as a journalist and been taught to have an inquiring mind and to probe below the surface, I would have reached the same conclusions that some of my African colleagues reached.

I came to the U.S. with an open mind. What I have written in this book will come as a shock to all of my friends in Ghana and the people who knew me there, who always identified me with Whites.

The so-called acceptance of Africans (I call it patronization) is not the only factor which has failed to endear us to the Black American. I reached a point where I could no longer keep my temper under control every time Blacks asked me why we Africans looked down on them.

They were looking at the problem from their angle. They did not know that many other Africans as well as myself had characterized Black Americans as unfriendly.

Peggy, a young White friend of mine, invited me to cocktails one Sunday afternoon. All the other guests were White, young and intelligent, but people with whom a Black person can feel at ease. Nevertheless, I still felt like the proverbial "spook who sat by the door." An hour or so later the doorbell rang. Peggy opened the door. Another young White man entered, followed by a Black man later introduced as Charles. I felt relieved not only because there was another Black face, but because Charles had that kind of commanding personality which makes it absolutely impossible for you to ignore him. He was not loud. He was not arrogant.

I sat there waiting patiently for the opportunity to break away from the general conversation, and to get to know him. Before that opportunity his White friend announced that they had to leave. I was so determined to get to know Charles that three days after our meeting, I called Peggy and asked for his number.

Charles wasn't home when I called, but someone was. I left a message for him. He did not return that call. A month later, Peggy had another get-together. I run into Bob, Charles' friend.

"How's Charles?" I asked him.

"You know, Fred, Charles thinks you don't like him." He replied.

"Why?" I asked, shocked.

"He mentioned it the night we left here. He said you did not say one word to him. He said that for some reason you Africans don't like Black Americans."

I called Charles a week later, and asked him to come to a luncheon I was giving for three Black students from Georgetown University who were going to Ghana for the summer. He agreed to come to the luncheon at 12:30. At eleven-thirty Charles called to say he was afraid he could not come. He had a bad hangover. We set a new date, again for a Sunday at seven. At seven fifteen the telephone rang. Again Charles said curtly, "Fred, I am afraid I cannot make it."

This incident was not an isolated one. Diplomats are generally thought of as hypocrites, especially in the art of cultivating friends. You are expected to move within certain circles no matter how loathesome you find some of the people. I refused to be caught up in this. If there were and are people I find pompous, loud or uninteresting, I couldn't care less who they were. I found many simple, ordinary people that I liked. Unfortunately, most of the young Blacks I reached out for never returned the gesture.

Blacks accuse African diplomats of socializing with only Whites. Maybe so, but what nobody is complaining about is that in a city like Washington, with a predominantly Black population, there is not one single hospitality program for African diplomats and students organized by the Blacks.

As I have pointed out, some African diplomats and students are prejudiced about Blacks. Their opinions are based on warnings given by Whites when they first arrive in America. What is more, many of the African embassies in Washington are located in predominantly Black areas. We tend to see all the faults of the Black man. We assume that all Blacks live and behave the way the people we see everyday do. The Black middle class has made little effort in counteracting the image which has been built of Blacks by some Whites. So we end up with a situation where some of the African diplomats and students return to their respective countries thinking that Blacks are responsible for their plight.

Those who refuse to accept the view that Blacks are responsible for their plight arrive at such conclusions because they have their minds, eyes and ears wide open. If they had to wait for a sincere friendship with Blacks to help them dispel some of the myths, they would wait till doomsday because for so many of them the opportunity to know Blacks never exists.

Just as American Blacks mistake White patronization of Africans for acceptance so it is that they also take our quietness for arrogance. African culture dictates that at a first meeting with people you wait to be talked to. You are considered forward if you go around introducing yourself to people. Everytime you meet Africans at parties they are either by themselves or standing alone in corners. They wait for people to talk to them. Once the ice is broken the friendship can develop, but Black Americans take this reserve for haughtiness. I knew, of course, that many I met did not actually intend to be unfriendly. It was just that like White Americans, they were all so deeply buried in the acquisition of material objects that they had little or no time for friendship. I could count any number of young Blacks I met that I wished I could have seen more of.

I do not deny that some of the African diplomats and

students in America enjoy the preference given them over American Blacks by Whites. I have heard Africans callously call Blacks "slaves" in the middle of an altercation. Similarly, I have heard Blacks who referred to Africans as "jungle men." Political immaturity and a lack of awareness are largely responsible for this name-calling and our inability to sympathetically look at each other's problems.

For too long the American Black had accepted the White man's propaganda that Africans were jungle people. They had no civilization. In his dealing with the African, the American Black has always felt superior. Some knowledgeable people feel that this attitude on the part of the Black American seems to have changed considerably since the independence of many of the African nations. That shame which Blacks associated with Africa has now been substituted with a certain amount of pride. It is even said by some that the emergence of the African nations had somehow intensified the civil rights movement in America.

But there are still millions of American Blacks who do not want to be identified in any way with Africa.

Among the batch of letters delivered at the Ghana Embassy one day in April 1970 was one which clearly explains how some Black minds have been confused. It was written by a Black woman in the Bronx, New York, to the Director of Mail Classification, Post Office Department, Bureau of Finance and Administration, Washington.

To be able to appreciate the contents of the letter

and the view in which it was written, some background information is necessary. The writer and her White friends had made the acquaintance of a Ghanaian Catholic priest while he was studying for a masters degree in education at Fordham University. The priest evidently had discussed with his American friends some of the financial problems which faced him in his missionary work. He won some sympathy.

After his return home, these friends would enclose small donations of five or ten dollars in their Christmas cards to the priest. Anyone should know that enclosing money in a letter to any part of the world is not only a risk, it is also illegal in many countries. In any case, the writer of the letter learned that the five-dollar bill she enclosed never reached the priest. I will now reproduce excerpts from the letter to show you the price that Ghana and the Black race paid for the stolen money:

"I hope you are not deceived by the Ghana postal authorities into believing that they had a law against cash being sent into the country. There is no doubt in my mind that the law was passed and made retroactive after you made inquiries. The money was seized August 1, 1969.

"Some years ago Secretary-General U Thant characterized some of the African leaders as CLOWNS. So true in this instance. Money was never stolen when Great Britain ruled the country. Ghana wants to borrow $15 million from us. I hope we do not lend them one penny. We do not have to become involved with unscrupulous people. And incidentally, so they will not be crying that

America is anti-Black, I happen to be a colored woman and I am mighty glad my ancestors on the colored side were brought to this country in chains. Of course, like most of us I have English blood too for which I am more than grateful. I just do not understand those Africans."

The more we try to educate our people's minds, the more we try to say to both Blacks and Africans: "Look, you are one people with one destiny," the more we find the U.S. press fighting hard against that issue.

In a series of articles dispatched from the West and East coasts of Africa in the fall of 1969, the *Washington Post* correspondent in Africa created the impression that a larger proportion of the Africans he had met in his travels and talked to on the race issue were sympathetic, but that overall Africans did not think they had anything in common with American Blacks. These four articles were published at a time when the embassy's speaking engagements were at a peak. In every Black school or college where I spoke, questions regarding the article featured prominently. At the Roosevelt Senior High School and Calvin Coolidge High School, both in the Northwest section of Washington, the articles dominated the discussions.

Quite a few young Black students in Washington where I lectured after the series was published were so upset that they looked for a scapegoat. They found one in me. They literally heckled me without any consideration for age and position.

The White American correspondent in Africa discovers to his delight something that the Black American visitor finds to his shock—trust in White people. In spite of the fact that both the African and the Black American have had histories of White domination, the African still has more faith, respect and trust in the White man than the Black man does. The reason is obvious. The Black American after the abolition of slavery still continues with the struggle of begging for a decent deal. He sees the White man as his oppressor.

If I, or any other Ghanaian, could not obtain employment, decent education, decent housing or a job, it is not because I was being denied any of these on the grounds of the color of my skin. My rival is another Black man. He is either more qualified than I am, or somebody is playing politics or nepotism. I live in a country where in spite of all its troubles, everyone has, at least, a sense of belonging; where the subject of race does not become an additional burden to a man's other problems.

I cannot recall any incident or story told to me by older members of my family which suggests that Africans have suffered under the White man the same inhuman treatment that the Black Americans have suffered since their arrival on American shores. The British held my country under subjugation for 103 years. They exploited its natural resources, but with exception of the governor and a few White administrators who remained on our soil as symbols of His Majesty's Government, everyone around us was Black.

The joke along the West Coast of Africa is that the

climatic conditions of West Africa, plus the anopheles mosquitoes, dissuaded the colonials from having any permanent designs on the countries there. Other than that, West Africans would have had to resort to the same bloody struggle for independence as the Kenyans did.

These are basic factors that anyone who tries to make comparisons between Africans and Black Americans cannot afford to ignore. Perhaps if the U.S. State Department had known this and had properly briefed Vice President Agnew, all of us would have been spared the embarrassment he caused himself with his famous speech on African and Black leaders.

In the summer of 1968, CBS rendered the whole Black world what I thought was a disservice. It sent to Ghana four young Blacks to stay with families there. The idea ostensibly was to give the young people a feel of the African way of life. Between New York and Accra, officials of the Ghana government worked hard to make the stay successful. On their return home the kids were interviewed on CBS.

One of them stubbornly said that she was horrified to find that slavery was still practiced in Ghana. Her argument was that she did not see the reason for sending Ghanaian young people to live with other relatives or strangers. What she could not accept was the service there young people provide to their host families. She called this slavery. She is guilty of misunderstanding a Ghanaian custom.

My brother and I lived away from home for two

years. We were not sent away because our parents could not afford to feed or clothe or educate us. Ghanaians believe that when a child grows up in a home where everything is available to him, he grows up without knowledge of the suffering of other people. We were sent away from home to live with less fortunate members of the family. We had to serve instead of being served by other young people who had been sent, in turn, to live with our family to learn how to do certain things.

Was CBS being unfair? I believe so, for the American youths had no understanding of Ghanaian culture. How could they explain it to other Americans?

In April 1969 one of Washington's television stations informed the embassy that it had decided to feature Ghana in one of its children's programs. We consented. An hour after I appeared on the program, a White friend of mine, a Southerner who knew I was to be on the program, called me at the office: "Fred Hayford, I am ashamed of you," he began.

"Why?" I asked.

"Do you know that the cartoon which was shown on the program this morning had a racial slur? It was a take-off on southern Blacks. Anyway, I thought I might warn you before any protests to the embassy are made. Pray that not many Blacks from the deep South saw it."

It turned out that only one professor from Howard University called our attention to it. How many of those who saw the program noticed the implication I do not know.

A Ghanaian student walked over to my office one morning. Her story was that she had been invited to appear on a television program which would discuss the "Afro" hairdo. "The point is, I am to make it clear to the Blacks here that we in Africa do not wear the Afro, that wearing the Afro to identify with Africa is wrong."

"I don't see where I come in," I told the young woman.

"I am Ghanaian, yes, but how do I know what women in other African countries do? I don't want to make a fool of myself so I decided to come here and check with you."

I could have thrown my arms around her. It would be a sweeping generalization for any African, let alone a foreigner, to say that the Afro is un-African. The styles vary. In South Africa, Rhodesia, and in some East African countries women do not plait their hair the way most women in West Africa do. Among the Ewes of Ghana, women wear their hair short. I grant anyone that the "Afro" as worn in Africa does not come anywhere near the size of the one being worn in America, but at the same time we must not overlook the fact that no African woman would want to wear her hair so bushy in eighty-five degree weather every day of her life.

Why do so many Whites get uptight every time Blacks claim identity with Africa?

On a cold winter day in New York, I stood for hours on Fifth Avenue, watching the St. Patrick's Day Parade. Irish-Americans were proudly displaying their cultural links with the motherland. I saw Poles, Italians, and Puerto Ricans do the same on different occasions. Nobody had a word against it. The only complaint has been the cost of cleaning the streets after the parades. People jam the pavements on Fifth Avenue each time there is such an ethnic celebration.

You go to a Chinese restaurant, an Italian or French one. Invariably, everybody from the manager right down to the waiter is Chinese American, Japanese American, Italian American or French American. But the minute an American Black claims identity with Africa, which is a historical fact, people question the validity of the claim.

The African embassies do not help the situation when they shrink from anything that brings them into close contact with Black Americans.

None of the other embassies will have second thoughts, for instance, about a request from their constituencies to use embassy facilities for a benefit. In the African diplomatic corps, certain ambassadors think that they should either clear such requests with the State Department or reject them outright. Some even refuse to take groups of Blacks on a tour of their embassies. This, they fear, would mean involvement in American politics! Meanwhile, the same diplomat probably complains bitterly that some of the worst questions on Africa come from Blacks. How and where these diplomats expect Blacks to learn about Africa, I do not know.

There is at least one American who admits that Africans and Black Americans are cousins. That person is

William Lanco of the American Nazi party. In separate but identical letters to all African ambassadors in Washington on August 17, 1970, Mr. Lanco said: "Go back to Africa, you stinking Black cannibals. You Negroes used to eat people in Africa. That's why we made slaves out of you niggers a hundred years ago—because you are cannibals. Get your dirty-Black asses out of this country, and take all these wire-haired cousins of yours with you. Get out."

Before my departure from Ghana, I had had a very close relationship with a number of Americans working either for the State Department or the Peace Corps. For some reason, three-quarters of the Americans I met were either from the Mid-West or California. One day a boy from Wisconsin volunteered an explanation: "Fred, the Mid-West is God's own country. If you meet any American who is not from the Mid-West, forget it. He's not important."

A young woman from San Francisco said, "If ever you're in California, Fred, go to San Francisco. Women there are beautiful and chic. The people of Los Angeles are sloppy." Likewise, snooty Washingtonians make jokes about North Carolinians.

In my own country and, I believe, in a host of others, you do come across such half-joking banter. You can always find one ethnic group that considers itself superior to the other ethnic groups. But the racism, the hate, the prejudice and the provincialism I found in America was unbelievable. I had not expected that in a society with such a high rate of affluence, education, sophistication and supposed religious fervor, people would have such bitterness and hate against a people who through no fault of their own have been born Black. Hypocrisy stops millions from coming out in the open to share Mr. Lanco's feelings. I admire him. At least I can deal with him.

The attitude of the majority of Whites I saw in Salt Lake City made me appraise the race problem in the U.S. My conclusions were that perhaps if there were not "too many" Blacks in the country, the need for contempt of the Black race would not arise.

Salt Lake was one of the few American cities I visited that has a very small number of Blacks. I could count on my hands the number of Black faces I saw. I stood in a heavy snowstorm on one corner in the outskirts of the city waiting for a bus. At least five drivers stopped and offered to drive me to wherever I was going.

Salt Lake has its evil people, too. The Mormons who control the city, I was warned, were no "Nigger lovers." But I cannot say that I found there the same contempt and hostility with which Blacks are treated in many parts of the U.S.A.

Las Vegas, another city which has very few Blacks, almost made me change the appraisal I had made in Salt Lake. I was sitting on a stool in front of a slot machine at the "Stardust." After three trials, sixty cents in dimes came out of the machine. Someone behind me drawled. "He must be one of them smart Niggers."

In the men's room in another casino, someone remarked "You can't go anywhere these days without being followed by Niggers, dope addicts and pimps."

Maybe all these experiences were good for me. My Black consciousness was being raised. Before, in a country where Whites were once idealized, I had unconsciously imitated Europeans. After experiencing a country where I was in the minority, it was possible to see my race and its struggles in a new perspective.

I knew I would go back to Ghana with a new sense of pride in being Black. But I was still unsure of how most Black Americans viewed Africans—and whether they felt any real kinship with Africa at all.

6

More Than Skin Deep

What are the characteristics common to both Africans and Black Americans? This dearth of information on whether or not such common characteristics exist, and if so what has influenced them, has led to some arguments. I met American Whites who assert outright that Africans are very different from American Blacks. I also met American Blacks of different economic backgrounds and ages who sneered at any comparison between themselves and Africans.

It is said that "when in Rome do as the Romans do." My Rome was America. I found that Americans, women especially, had the habit of addressing their equals as "girl." Black women would refer to grown-ups as "child." With Black men the references were "cat" or "guy." White men would often refer to men as "boys."

I decided against the use of "cat" or "guy." They sounded too slangy-American to me. I chose the word "boy." In no time at all, I was informally referring to all of my friends in my age group and below as "boys." My White friends raised no objection to this reference. The Black ones did.

I was at a loss. Why were my young Black friends being so fussy over a term? A few months later, a young Black woman offered an explanation. During slavery and after abolition, southern Whites contemptuously referred to every Black man, regardless of age, as "boy." The term had therefore become derogatory as far as the Black man was concerned. Every Black male, no matter what his age, insists on being called a man. It is his sensitive spot. I understood the explanation, but I still thought that American Blacks were being unnecessarily jumpy on such a trivial issue.

Soon afterwards, a White woman unconsciously made me aware that I should have had better sense than to have harbored that feeling against American Blacks.

The vice-chancellor of the University of Ghana, Dr. Alex Kwapong, was invited by the Smithsonian Institute in Washington to chair a symposium entitled "Man and Beast—A Comparative Social Behavior" in 1969. This was a time when I thought that Blacks all over the world should prove something to the world (I no longer think they should. Now I think they should be themselves). The fact that a Black man had chaired the symposium meant so much to me that I wanted to give the widest coverage of the function in the "Ghana News," of which I was editor.

As I browsed through the set of photographs sent to me by the Smithsonian, I came upon one which I found revolting, but which to any American, Black or White, would have seemed perfectly normal. In the photograph was a line-up of the officials who had worked on the plans for the symposium together with Dr. Kwapong and another Ghanaian. Among the officials was a White woman who carried a chimpanzee in her arms. There could be no doubt that she had carried that chimp simply because that was what the symposium had been about—comparative studies between man and beast.

That knowledge still did not stop me from being insulted by the woman's action. During the colonial era, it was not uncommon for British administrative officers to compare Ghanaians with monkeys. When an Englishman was irritated by a Ghanaian, he would say, "You Black monkey." There was the famous case of an Anglican bishop who was said to have taken a photograph of a Ghanaian boy with a monkey beside him. The photograph was mailed to friends in London under the caption "Two Monkeys."

That association of ideas crept into my mind when I saw that Smithsonian photograph. Just as any Black man in the U.S. objects to any reference of "boy" because of unpleasant past experiences, so it is that the Ghanaian becomes insulted at the mere display of a monkey by a

White person. At least the African and the Black man have one thing in common.

When my friend Gary was home from school and was visiting me, we got into a heavy discussion about what Gary calls my socio-religious background. He thought it had made me a prude. On this particular occasion, Gary was so determined to make me change my views on what constitutes morality that even when I left him in the living room and went into the shower he continued with the discussion. He could not hear me while the water was running so he moved closer to the bathroom. I had to shout to make myself audible.

When I finally came out of the shower and started to apply grease to my body, Gary looked at me and said, "You sure are a nigger indeed."

"Why?" I asked.

"Why?" "Why are you putting all that grease on your body?"

"Because my skin turns white if I don't," I replied, especially around this time of the year."

"Fred, you try too hard not to be a nigger, but that's what you are. On Connecticut Avenue you can call it 'white' but on the other side of town we call it 'ash'—'niggers' ash'. All Black folks in this country have that problem, but I didn't think Africans had it too."

Suddenly I remembered that a British lady who had taught me English in high school had once remarked in class that the reason Africans use grease on their bodies was simply because they wanted their bodies to shine.

That statement was false. All the boys in the class knew the lady did not know what she was talking about and yet not one of us challenged her or corrected that false impression. Now Gary had made me aware that the "ash" was not only akin to Africans but to the whole Black race.

It seems to me, however, that there are many, many more similarities which exist between the African Black and his American cousin.

I compare the status and role of the American woman to the African woman, and I ask myself what precisely does the American woman mean when she talks about liberation. At the risk of incurring the displeasure of women's liberationists I daresay that what the American woman is asking for is over-liberation.

The African woman has no control over the finances of her husband. Her husband is an absolute ruler. He decides how much money should be spent on food, or in Ghanaian parlance "Chop money." If she runs short, too bad.

In spite of this, the Ghanaian woman would economize to such an extent that she would still have enough left over to buy herself a few tubes of bleaching cream. She may be beautiful or ugly. Her man accepts her for what she is, but she is not satisfied with her looks. All extra coppers go into the bleaching creams. It has been built into her mind that the fairer she looks the more beautiful she is. All through her education this concept has been impressed upon her. She ends up with a fair face and a Black body.

I have seen women who would apply to their faces all day very harsh antiseptic soaps. By the time they are ready to wash the soap off their faces, they are so sore that the application of water has to be done gently. After a week or two the desired lighter effect is achieved. I also know of mothers who pound together three or more harsh indigenous and imported antiseptic soaps to wash their babies' skin, so that the babies would develop lighter skins.

I have played and seen other Ghanaian youngsters play a game in which all assembled bring their arms together for a judge to see who has the fairest arms in the group. Before the judge's opinion, each participant shouts: "Look at it carefully. Can't you see I am your White man?"

In the U.S. it was the same. In many bathrooms of the Black woman, the familiar tube was there—the bleaching cream.

My cousin Josephine is an intelligent, well-educated woman. I was talking to her at one time about a boy she was serious about, but whom nobody in the family seemed to care for. In conversation with her one evening, I broached the subject. Josephine offered me an honest explanation. The boy she wanted to marry was light-skinned. There was a strong possibility, she told me, that their children would be light-skinned, too. Ribbons would go very well on their hair—a beautiful exhibition of how we have lost our identity.

I am told that at the time Washington's Howard University was founded, it was impossible for dark people like me to gain admission there. You had to be light before your application would be considered.

The "in thing" to do when I was in my third year in high school was to concoct a mixture of egg yolks, raw potatoes and some chemicals stolen from the school laboratory, and apply it to the hair. The hair turned silky after the application. We then swept through the hair a hot comb. All in the name of looking White.

At the same high school one of my English teachers, born in Barbados, brought up and educated in the U.S. and now living in Ghana, assigned us an oral composition, "What I intend to be when I leave school." One of the boys surprised everybody by saying he would migrate to Jamaica to become a fisherman. In a country where fishing is considered menial, no one clearly understood why Tony, the best student in class, would want to do something like that!

But the teacher had her own reason to be shocked at Tony. She told us that Jamaica had a terrible caste system. If Tony, who was as dark as I am, ever migrated to Jamaica, the prejudices against dark-skinned people might jeopardize his happiness. Our jaws dropped. Jamaica is a Black country.

As it is in many other lands, fruits in Ghana do come in different species. Who named these fruits I do not know, but if a Ghanaian fruit has a soft, velvety texture then there is a prefix—European banana, European orange, European apple. If it is plain and rough, naturally it becomes a plain banana or orange.

In Denver, Colorado, I was told so much about the magnificent scenery between that state and California that I ultimately elected to continue my journey to San Francisco by train. I had the time, besides, I wanted to see as much of America as I possibly could.

On my arrival at the Denver railway station, accompanied by a Ghanaian friend, we asked and were told on which platform to board the train. Six White passengers had formed a queue at the time we arrived there. On the ground was an elderly Black man. He took the suitcases of all the White passengers and helped them board the train.

It was soon my turn. He looked sheepishly at me but did not make a move to take my suitcase.

"Yeah, there's a proper Negro. Old as air and twice as polluted," I thought, borrowing one of Moms Mabley's lines. The thought of that man treating me differently enraged me. Without thinking, I pushed my heavy suitcase into the old man's hand and boarded the train.

"What in the world made you do that?" Osei, my friend, questioned.

"If he is paid to handle the luggage of White passengers, he is paid to handle mine, too," I retorted.

I made three layovers. Between San Bernardino and Riverside, I used the diner for the first time. The elderly Black stewards were pitiful. I admire any man working for a wage, but what I saw in that diner was sickening. Elderly

Black men were unnecessarily playing subservient roles. The "Yes, Sirs" and "Yes, Ma'ams" were enough to make me sick. They hovered over the White patrons and engaged in long conversations.

One of the stewards, bringing a cold plate to a White woman who sat at my left, suddenly broke into a song: "I found my thrill on Blueberry Hill." Encouraged by some of the Whites, our friend displayed his rich, baritone voice by singing two more verses of the song. I knew that man was working towards a fine tip. When the woman finally left, our friend found she had left not a penny on the table. Our eyes met. I broke into laughter and ran out of the diner before he could vent his spleen on me.

However, it could be said that White waiters are often equally subservient and with the same end in sight— a fat tip.

I have told this story because it brings to memory instances in Ghana where postal store clerks would give immediate service to Whites, favoring them over Ghanaians. Until Ghanaians raised an uproar over it, some postal clerks would ask a White person, even if he were third or last in a queue, to come forward for service while the Ghanaian was kept waiting. Store clerks would keep other shoppers waiting while they neatly packed groceries and other provisions of Whites. A Ghanaian customer was handed a bag to do his own packing.

I observed in America, just as I had observed in Ghana, that our people enjoy making worthless, unproductive investments. On both the working class and middle class levels, the Black American woman, without doubt, was more elegantly dressed than her White counterpart. Black American and African women surely spend more per capita on clothes than do White women. The question is: Can the Black women afford it? Definitely not. They do it to prove something.

Just as the average American Black woman invests so much in clothes to play a subconscious game of "Anything you can do I can do better," so the average Black man's main consideration in life often is a car he can ill afford. These investments are mocked by Whites. But when a man has been denied the good things of life for so long a time, he makes wasteful investments once that denial is lifted. This may also explain why Blacks have not yet joined the revolution by young Whites to reject materialism. The White youths have had a taste of the "good life." They have learned that materialism does not necessarily make a person any happier but rather tends to make a slave out of a human being. It makes a man greedy. Blacks and Africans have not yet made this discovery. We are taking over where the Whites are leaving off.

The only characteristic for which I cannot blame any White person is what is known in the U.S. as C.P.T. (Coloured Peoples Time) and known in Africa as African Punctuality. You invite the average African or Black person to dinner or a party. If the dinner is for eight o'clock tell him it's at six-thirty.

When Ghana Airways first introduced Ghanaian pilots on its domestic and international flights, Ghanaians were so skeptical about the ability of their own men to control the engines that they made excuses to travel on foreign-owned planes. Even politicians who made the most vitriolic attacks against colonialism and neo-colonialism cleverly avoided Ghana Airways planes.

At the time that I was leaving Ghana, the medical school there was in the throes of producing its first doctors. It would not surprise me in the least if on my return home I learned that Ghanaians had their reservations about these. A foreign-trained Ghanaian doctor could be known to be a "magister cum libris"—without his books he cannot diagnose any disease—but so long as he is known to have been trained in a foreign country, especially a Western one, the Ghanaians will place him on a pedestal.

One would think that the majority of Africans who have studied or lived in foreign countries and have followed the political and social development of these countries would return home with the understanding that even the most sophisticated and advanced nations are not infallible in their policies and decisions.

They do not. Over and over we hear "Oh Africans, we have a long way to go," "such a thing would never happen in any Western country," and "no civilized nation would do that." Yes, many Africans, both the elite and the ordinary men, measure civilization in terms of industrial progress. You cannot blame them. They are reflecting the views of their Western-oriented education.

In assessing the conduct of their own government or

other African governments, many educated Africans are uncharitable. We have learned at school what this or that Western government did at a certain time in its history, so we expect our governments to do likewise. We read what Western newspapers and magazines think of our own governments and we base our own opinions on them forgetful of the fact that our values are often diametrically opposed to Western values.

There are other similarities I have found existing between Africans and Black Americans. For instance, another member of the embassy staff and I were so deeply struck by the facial resemblance of many of the Blacks we saw to Africans that each time we tried to place them in one of the ethnic groups of Ghana. A few times we disagreed, but generally we concurred that the ancestors of the Black person we had seen were either Fantis, Ashantis, Ewes, Gas or Hausas.

Some of the Blacks seemed delighted when they learned of the resemblance. Others were surprised to hear our comment. I myself was taken aback the day a young Black man walked by me with the words, "Hi, my African brother."

"How do you know?" I asked.

"By your walk. You Africans always walk erect." I had never thought of that before. I did not even know we walk differently.

I have noticed that to some extent Blacks share with their African cousins the same concern over families and the same closeness which exists in African families. Unlike Whites, many Black families do not think it is strange for young men and women to live home and work at the same time. Whites give me the impression that once a son or daughter makes his own living he should be on his own. What also impresses me about Black families is the presence of old people in the home. Coming from a culture where no old peoples' homes exist, it bothers me each time I walk past such an institution or hear a friend say he is visiting his father or mother in a home. It seems like neglect of one's parents or grandparents.

Another similarity is the Black man's gargantuan appetite for women. It is interesting to note that while the American Black woman cries her woes in "blues," her African cousin cries in the "Adenkum." They all complain it is a man's world. I refuse to be caught up in the argument about the virility of African Black men, but I do not mind agreeing that African Black men are hot blooded.

Attitudes of the African Black women to interracial marriages, I have observed, differ slightly. The African woman whose son, brother or uncle marries a foreign woman while he is studying abroad, accepts this marriage as inevitable. Even so she will work towards its break-up if she finds the opportunity. Her lack of enthusiasm for this marriage is not determined by her hostility towards Whites or foreigners. It is cultural.

I know that my sister is very uptight about the possibility of my being married to an American, Black or White. In every letter I send her I make sure I mention the name of an American girl I am going with. She knew I had an intendant in Ghana so it did not worry her when I told her of the other girls. When my intended changed her mind and got engaged to another boy, my sister became enraged when I announced that I had a good reason to marry the daughter of a rich White. It was not true. I just enjoyed the reaction the announcement would produce. She wrote back threatening to ask the Ministry of Foreign Affairs to recall me if I insisted on the marriage.

An American Black woman may have been motivated to resort to this action out of the hostility and suspicion bred by America's race relations.

Like other Ghanaian women, my sister expresses concern and opposition to my being married to a foreigner since such marriages invariably destroy the relationships between a mother and son, a sister and brother or even a brother and brother. Under present Ghanaian conditions members of a family would always make a contribution no matter how small for the education and needs of one another. The idea is to help someone to help others in the future. This is beautifully illustrated by a proverb in which a father says to his child: "I will be responsible for your upkeep till all your teeth are fully grown. Then you will be responsible for me until all my teeth are out."

My sister may never need any financial assistance from me. Nevertheless she sees a union between me and a non-Ghanaian woman as a threat to our relationship. At one point in her life, every Ghanaian woman, no matter how quiet she is, tells members of her family some of her marital and financial problems. If my sister was visiting me she could discuss her problems with me without my Ghanaian wife being in the way. This is because during such visits, the wives understand the need of the husbands to be alone with their mother or sister at certain times. They excuse themselves without being asked or told. From experience, the foreign woman always feels she has a right to be by her husband's side. Also while the Ghanaian woman may begrudge frequent visits of her in-laws, but would put on a happy face during the visit, foreign women cannot restrain themselves from making it clear that they do not approve of such visits.

In the U.S. interracial dating and marriages is frowned upon by Blacks for an entirely different reason. In the heat of a discussion one day in New York, Brenda, the daughter of my "adopted parents," said "Fred, if you ever start going with a White girl, stop knocking on our doors. Washington has more Black girls than they know what to do with."

At the time I was hurt, but in Washington I discovered that Brenda could have saved her breath, and that I could have spared myself the pain her statement caused me. For one thing Washington was not prepared for was interracial dating and marriage.

The antagonism is clearly visible on the faces of both races. Some Americans dislike interracial association so intensely that even walking or driving through their neighborhood with a White man can be perilous. An English lady who works as a telephone operator in the embassy lives near me so I often give her a ride home. On days that traffic is very heavy on 16th Street, I make a detour which takes me into 17th Street and Columbia Road, a neighborhood heavily populated by Blacks and Puerto Ricans. The looks, as I drive through the neighborhood on any summer day with the residents sitting on their stoops, are evil. The comments are obscene.

Had I lived in Ghana all my life, the chances are that I might have married a White girl without a second thought. After my American experience, the possibility is ruled out. The decision no longer becomes mine. It is the business of other people, both Black and White.

If I had lived in Ghana all my life, I would have picked up things accidentally dropped by White people or opened doors for White women I had never met before, because I consider them a part of mankind. In America I would not, because color immediately creeps into my mind. It's a sad, sad way of life.

Some fallacies still exist in interracial dating and marriage. Black women, for instance, assume that once a Black man marries a White woman he has rejected his own kind. Many of us also assume that a White man married to a Black woman has liberated himself from prejudices. We do not seem to be aware that once you bring people of different sexes together you are bound to have a natural reaction. It just happens that some people are able to resist this natural reaction more than others. I do not think that one can generalize that every Black man, successful or not, who is married to a White woman is a traitor to the cause. Neither can we generalize that any White man married to a Black woman is free of prejudice. It's either for love or convenience.

The tragedy about this question as to whether a Black man can marry a White woman or vice-versa is that after a while, I find myself so caught up in the argument against it that no matter how attractive a White woman is, I can not look at her as a woman. My relations with White women are strictly on a friendly basis. I can not be involved with one either emotionally or physically. I have been influenced so much so that my deep friendship with a Ghanaian eventually became cool. This friend never visited me without being followed by his White girl friend. To avoid hurting his feelings, I hid the truth from him. I told him that I did not particularly care for his coming to my apartment with his White girl friend because it always meant our conversing in English. There was another Ghanaian friend who had a different White girl each time I saw him. One day when I broached the subject, he replied, "These women should pay the colonial debts. The sins of the fathers must be visited upon the children."

I parked Bob's car in front of the Greyhound Station in Montgomery, Alabama. Bob, my friend and traveling companion in the South, had been delayed in Atlanta, Georgia, and had not been able to drive with me as we had planned. By the time I arrived in Montgomery I was hungry. The thought of entering any restaurant to be told that I would not be served, and the injustice of the whole race question, made me feel evil. I figured that in the Greyhound cafeteria, no one could deny me service—if they carry Blacks on their buses, surely they could serve us in their cafeteria, too. I walked into the cafeteria. Only two of the customers were White. The rest were all Black. I thought it was funny to have a White cashier and waitress in a restaurant patronized by Blacks in a place like Alabama. I approached the White cashier and ordered the day's special, a southern meal, whatever that was.

Ten minutes later she placed before me a plate of grits and two thick slices of ham swimming in red-eye gravy. I tasted the grits. They were buttery. Just then, a young Black man of about fourteen or fifteen walked to the juke box and inserted a dime. Two seconds later, Aretha Franklin came out with "Call Me." What a coincidence! Here I was sitting in a restaurant in Montgomery, Alabama, eating grits and ham and someone was waiting in Atlanta, Georgia, for me to call.

Before I could make up my mind whether to reach for the phone or finish my first truly southern meal, the boy walked straight to my table, took my hand, and gave me the Black Panther handshake.

I was overwhelmed by his friendship. Nowhere in the North, not even in the so-called city of brotherly love, Philadelphia, had I experienced such warmth. Black men walk past you in many northern cities and say "Hi, Brother," but without as much as a smile. It was so perfunctorily done that it never impressed me.

As bad as race relations in the South are, if I had to spend the rest of my life in the U.S., I have no doubt in my mind that I would choose to live in the South. I made four trips to the deep South. My friends in the North were puzzled as to why I kept going back. The truth of the matter was that the Blacks I met there have not as yet lost that natural touch that makes a person's heart and soul beautiful. Southern Whites who have learned to live in peaceful co-existence with us are no less beautiful. I would hate to see the day that industrialization would destroy the beautiful living patterns of southerners.

I can never forget the day I was awakened from my sleep in a Greyhound bus in Baton Rouge, Louisiana, by a young Black boy:

"Hi, you doing all right?"

"Yes, why?" I asked sleepily.

"You been sleeping too long."

His face showed real concern, but how do you explain to a seven-year-old boy, Black or White, that you had stayed up all night on New Orlean's famous Bourbon Street and that you were sleeping to make up for what you missed the night before?

Neither can I forget the young Black man who waded knee-deep into the sea in Galveston Island, Texas, to embrace me when he learned from my White friends sitting on the beach that I was from Africa. A southern Black did not have to call me brother. The feeling was mutual—the experience worth having.

I also remember quite vividly my vacation on a farm

in Boonville, North Carolina, digging potatoes, picking strawberries, squash, string beans and tomatoes. I went to bed each night to the sound of crickets and woke up each morning to the woodpecker pecking at the window. I learned to eat an enormous breakfast: fried apples, homemade biscuits with homemade jam and fried ham. My string beans were cooked with fatback.

Within three days, I had shaken hands with every member of the family of the friend on whose invitation I had gone to Boonville. It was like going back to Elmina. The most touching moment was on the day of our departure. People woke up in the early hours of the morning to go to their farms to bring us fresh fruits and vegetables as gifts.

All these things went through my mind in the restaurant in Montgomery, Alabama. After his handshake, the young Black said to me: "Where are you heading to, man?"

"Houston, Texas. And you?"

"Mobile, Alabama."

"Oh, Mobile! Want a ride? I'm going there."

"Thank you very kindly, but I've to check on some folks down here first," he said. "I come from Mobile, but my parents sent me up North to go stay with my aunt in Chicago and go to school. Man, I am going back to Mobile. Folks in Chicago are killing everybody. Too many gangs up there."

I knew what he was talking about. The newspapers had been full of reports of gang killings, but I wanted to tell him it was not as bad there as he was saying.

I pointed out that in Mobile he had the worst enemy, the southern cracker—or red neck as White people might call him. At this, he jumped from his seat: "Yeah, but that's where I belong."

At that point, I wished I could have mounted him on the highest mountain in America. I would have given him the most powerful microphone to announce to all of Black America: "No peace, no peace. No peace anywhere. You do not solve a problem by running away from it. You fight that problem where it exists."

When Black Americans come to identify with Africa, I say "Right on." It is a historical fact no one can deny. Similarly, when they decide to go to Africa on vacation, I give them every encouragement. The African nations can do with the dollars that the Black middle class so shamelessly spend in Europe. When Blacks take up jobs in African countries to lend their technical support and expertise to the people, I cannot fail to show my appreciation.

I dissent, however, when Blacks talk about migration to Africa. I had to advise Blacks who came to the embassy to inquire about the possibilities of taking Ghanaian citizenship that they should initially take a job there and get to know the country and the people before coming to any such decision. I have my reasons for such a strong reservation on migration. I leave the social and other problems connected with such a move to the experts to deal with—I would like to deal with the subject on a personal basis.

Within the last three and a half years, I have found that it is most difficult for Americans to learn to appreciate other people's customs, habits and living conditions. Generations of Americans have become so used to the latest technology that they just cannot visualize how other people can live without this or that appliance or convenience. Other people's ways of life, therefore, become "primitive."

I had a friend whose daughter was in the Peace Corps in Africa. My friend's daughter loved it in Africa, but her mother could not see how she could live without a refrigerator or wash her clothes without hot water. Her fear was that the clothes would not come clean in cold water. The food kept out of a refrigerator, she feared, might go bad.

Refrigerators, gas ranges, washing machines, flush toilets, telephones, tap water and electricity, to name only a few, are basic necessities in the U.S. In Africa they are all luxury items. We have had cases of Black Americans visiting Ghana who were miserable outside the big cities, where such facilities were unavailable. They felt, and rightly so, that they had been cut off completely from their idea of civilization.

So far the only Black Americans who have felt comfortable in Ghana are those who have Ghanaian government or U.S. government jobs, and have had these conveniences provided by their respective governments, even in small towns. Once you take these away from them, they are as lost as the Ghanaian middle class city man who is visiting his former village.

There is also the problem of cultural differences. No Ghanaian woman deceives herself that her husband belongs to her alone. They all agree that "a man will always be a man"—in other words, he will play around. So long as he can keep his affair from the knowledge of his wife, he is safe. If the affair comes into the open, he is in trouble. She will not desert him or use that affair as grounds for divorce, but she will fight, physically if necessary, to break up the affair.

What we have seen in Ghana so far is that the Black American woman, like the Westerner that she is, sees the affair as an end to the love between her and her Ghanaian husband. She looks for the next available plane home. She does not see a fight for him as necessary. I do not blame her. She belongs to a society which views the situation differently.

Personally, I deplore this attitude of the American Black woman. She should know that the Black man wherever you find him—in Africa, the Caribbean and the U.S.—needs understanding. I do not say that she has to compromise with every situation, but she does not have to give up and flee in search of another man simply because her husband has had a harmless little affair.

My dissent on whether Blacks should migrate to Africa made me unpopular among some Black college students. Each time the subject came up some of the students got so emotional about it that they just wanted me to say what they wanted to hear. I tried to discuss some of the negative aspects of it. I was in a position to know that very, very few of the African governments have a clear-cut policy on U.S. Blacks. Mine, I know, encourages strong cultural ties. But it does not encourage migration. At Ohio State in Columbus, only a miracle saved me and the Black students from literally coming to blows because of my dissension.

Rather than making young Blacks prematurely look to Africa as the promised land, I think that Black leaders who pursue the matter vigorously should help in educating our people to learn more about each other and the problems that beset us before plunging us into a fruitless venture.

A lot of educating needs to be done on both sides. The American Black must have his facts correct on Africa. He does not need to wear any pretentious garb to make identity with Africa a reality.

In this regard, I think that Black universities should give serious consideration to the suggestion made by my ambassador, E. M. Debrah, to Clark College in Atlanta that there should be an exchange of students between African universities and Black American colleges and universities. Our people need that exposure to help them break down the myths and resolve the differences which exist between them.

On my visits to U.S. campuses, I became deeply interested in how education affects American racial frictions.

7

Witch Come and Take This Piece so that You Don't Kill My Child

(Ghanaian Proverb)

English is a second language to all Ghanaians. Children are first exposed to it in the first grade. But after years of studying it through the grade and high schools, many of us still find that we are not quite proficient in the language. We generally assume that we cannot speak it or write it the way the British or the Americans can. I was therefore completely horrified when I discovered that some Americans, particularly Blacks in the inner cities, not only do not have the command I thought they had, but made some errors that even Ghanaians would consider unforgivable.

Examples of these mistakes were "I should have took it," "Was you there?" "He does not want to do nothing," "They was talking to me." Each time I heard these, I tried to tell myself either that I had not heard very well or that my own imagination was running wild. But I kept hearing these disturbing sentences. The bad grammar plus poor spelling of Black youths became well known to me through my rounds of some of the inner-city schools in the District of Columbia, Maryland and Northern Virginia.

Prior to this, I had undertaken a similar speaking tour of some of the high schools on New York's Long Island and New Jersey's Bergen County. The number of Blacks in these area high schools was insignificant, but I had noticed that, unlike those I had met in some New York City public schools, their use of language was quite good.

Naturally, I was interested to know why there was such a deficiency in the cities. Did the kids make these errors and spell badly because they were, as we have been led to believe, not mentally as capable as Whites? If so, how was it that those I had met in the suburban schools in New York, New Jersey, Northern Virginia and Maryland spoke and wrote so well?

As I became more and more involved with American Blacks, I began to understand some of the factors which have led to this bad grammar in inner-city schools. One of the problems, in fact, also exists in Ghana and probably in many other African countries: I was taught English at school and was encouraged to speak it with my classmates during school. But the minute I arrived home, I spoke the language of my own people. There were not that many people who spoke fluent English, and even if there had been, why should they abandon their own language to speak one which was foreign to them?

The result is that the Ghanaian child comes to depend very heavily on the school for the development of his English. He has little or no help at home.

The problem in Nigeria is closer to that of Black America. At school the Nigerian student is taught the rudiments of the so-called "Queen's English," but outside the school he communicates with fellow Nigerians not through the Queen's English but through another medium known as pidgin English. Instead of the generally accepted "I am going," the Nigerian would say "Ah de go." "It is he" turns out to be "Na him" and "It is so" becomes "Na so." The Black American child also learns good English at school, but at home and in the neighborhood he runs into people who speak ghettoese.

Ghettoese has become traditional because the slaves on their arrival could not speak any English. No efforts were made to educate them, and, in fact, educating slaves was usually forbidden by law. They picked up what they could, and what they picked up has been passed down from generation to generation. Because Ghettoes has become accepted in inner cities, very few parents draw the attention of their children to its incorrectness.

I felt sick when business executives pointed out this

deficiency in Blacks as one of the factors which prevented any significant employment of Blacks in their companies or in government. Any time the subject cropped up at a private dinner party, the excuse was always the same: "We cannot find enough qualified Negroes to fill responsible positions."

I wondered whether people who make these claims saw what I saw, too.

With the mass migration of Whites into the suburbs, the enrollment in practically all of the schools in the inner cities and sometimes even in middle-class Black neighborhoods becomes what a friend of mine calls "93.3 percent." What this means, in effect, is that the great majority of the kids in the schools in the cities are Black. Unlike Ghana where parents have the right to send their children to any school they choose, in America there are restrictions on children going to schools outside their neighborhood. If the neighborhood is predominantly Black or White, then it follows that the school has a majority of Black or White kids. Poor White parents who live in an equally poor Black neighborhood have no choice but to send their children to the predominantly Black school. The insignificant number of poor Whites makes the school officially a desegregated one.

Similarly, schools in the suburbs become predominantly White. Very few Blacks can afford to move into the suburbs. Those who do send their children to the suburban schools. The few Black children help to make the suburban schools desegregated. In some of the suburban schools one cannot find a single Black face because that particular suburb has not been "desegregated" yet. So in practically the entire U.S. you have an imbalance of White and Black students in the schools.

This separation of the races at such an early age obviously does not allow any meaningful contact between the majority of Black and White children. Instead of learning about each other directly the kids learn about each other through their parents. It is here that the prejudices begin. The parents impart them to the children. White kids grow up with a morbid fear of Blacks. They have no way of determining for themselves whether the prejudices passed on to them by their parents are true or false. Their only admiration for the Black man and woman is in the field of sports and music, in which they see Blacks excel. In other spheres of life, a Black man is seen as a killer, a rapist, a drunkard. In short, a ne'er-do-well who should be kept at arm's length.

For many White kids the only time that they have their first real contact with Black people is either in college or at work. By this time, the damage is already done. The White has not learned to overcome his fear and distrust of the Black, and the Black has no real desire for a genuine friendship with someone who has kept him and his brother down.

For six months, I used one of Washington's top private schools to conduct an experiment in race relations among the youth. The reason this particular school was chosen was just because I had a "nephew" there—the son of a very good Black friend of mine. I had to pick up Kevin from school several times. It dawned on me that even though the students in that private school all had two things in common, middle-class background and brains, each time I went to pick up Kevin there was the same separation of races. The Black boys always stood in a group waiting for rides or the bus. The Whites stood in two's and three's or alone, waiting for their rides or the bus.

This may explain why I could not share the faith of many White parents who told me that the younger generation would be the ones to solve America's race problem. How do White youths, including the leaders of tomorrow, learn to appreciate the problems of Blacks when they are separated from them from infancy?

Two encounters with young people from the South have, however, given me some hope for the future. The first of these was in Philadelphia in 1969. I had gone to the city to help in the briefing of over a hundred Peace Corps volunteers who were going to Ghana for two-year teaching assignments.

I was in my hotel room reading one Friday night after supper when I heard a tap on my door. I opened it to see six of the White volunteers standing there. They were giving a "beer blast" on the roof top of the Hotel Sylvania. Would I care to join them?

I had never been very enthusiastic about parties given by White youths. Instead of swinging to take their minds from some of the problems and miseries of this world, they sat around and burdened themselves with long discussions on the same problems and miseries that one tries to escape at parties. Their parties generally had too much of a cocktail setting, but on that occasion I thought that a beer blast on a hotel roof top was better than being alone on a Friday night.

I accepted the invitation and followed them to the roof top. The introduction began:

"I am . . . from North Carolina."

"I am . . . from Georgia."

"I am . . . from Tennessee."

"I am . . . from North Carolina."

"I am . . . from Alabama."

"Oh, Lord!" I interrupted at that point. "It seems like I am in the wrong place!" There was silence all over. The expressions on their faces were sad.

"Why did you say that?" The girl from North Carolina asked me.

"I was only teasing," I defended myself.

"No, seriously, Mr. Hayford. We want you to be quite frank with us," she said.

I explained that I had never met a White person fresh from the South before, and that from what I had heard about the South I was wondering about the motive of the invitation. That remark brought the cat out of the bag. Although the youths had only two more days before emplaning to Ghana, they still entertained doubts as to what kind of reception would be accorded them if the Ghanaians heard that they were from the South! It took me

170

some time to convince them that in Ghana they would be accepted for what they were and not on the grounds of race, color or creed.

Never had I met a group of young Whites who were so deeply concerned about race relations in America and the future of the race question. The young lady from North Carolina confided she had given up trying to make her widowed mother see Blacks as human. Some of what the young people told me about their families' attitude toward Blacks was incredible. I came to suspect that one reason they had elected to join the Peace Corps was to escape from the strain and stress of racism. How do you deal with people who persistently call other people names and point out only their faults?

I discussed this issue with the-then Ghana Desk Officer at the Peace Corps. It turned out that she was already familiar with the problem in the Peace Corps. One of the volunteers from the deep South whose parents were hostile to Blacks had been assigned to Ghana by the Peace Corps without any previous knowledge of her background.

In Ghana she learned to see Ghanaians as people like herself. She mixed with them, learned about their faults and their good points. Eventually, she was able to rid herself of the fear which had been built into her mind about Blacks. When her assignment was over, however, the prospect of going back to the South to subjugate these same Black people, as the society there demanded, weighed so heavily on her mind that the poor girl had an emotional breakdown.

In Daytona Beach, Florida, I had another taste of how relations could be strained between prejudiced parents and broad-minded children.

I was deeply buried in thought in one corner of the beach when I heard a voice say "Hi." I looked up. There was a White youth, about sixteen. I was not particularly happy at the intrusion.

As I had walked over a three-mile stretch of beach, the Whites sitting on the beach or driving on the sands stared at me in a way I did not like. Not everyone, of course, had the look of "What are you doing here, Nigger?" Some were quietly admiring the outfit I had on which was made from African prints.

By the time I reached the part where I was lying in seclusion, I had been stared at so much that I had no desire to see another White face.

"You mind if I sit here and talk for a while?" the young White asked. In no time at all the boy had told me he was from Memphis, Tennessee, and had left home because of a breach with his parents over his friendship with a Black youth he had met at school.

I met teachers in the suburbs who almost went on their knees on my arrival in their schools to ask me to be brutally frank with the kids because they knew nothing about the problems of being Black. What the teachers told me was not far from the truth. Many White youths repeated to me the same old stereotyped images about

172

Blacks that their parents have held since time immemorial. They lack an understanding of the Black issue.

In some cases, they forgot the fact that I was an African and directed their questions about American Blacks at me. (1) What do the Blacks want? (2) Why don't they want to work hard? (3) Why are they so violent? (4) Why do they envy us so much?

More than half the buildings in which Black kids are educated from grade school through senior high are so depressing that any time I was invited to speak at any of these schools, I accepted the invitation rather reluctantly. These buildings were built at a time when the neighborhoods were all White. Now that the Whites have fled and the communities have become predominantly Black, it seems that nobody is properly maintaining these buildings and their equipment.

The contrast between them and those in the suburbs was so vast that I could not help wondering why there was such a disparity. The inner city school child sees so much depression in his life that if there is one thing he does not need it is a dingy, depressing environment at school. It saddens me, quite naturally, to see so many Black youths drop out from school, but maybe if I happened to be in their shoes I would do the same.

Pressure from Blacks and civil rights movements have led to a new policy which aims at achieving racial balance in schools through busing of pupils from a predominantly Black school to a White school or vice versa. The administration's opposition to busing has apparently been necessitated by the fear that most White parents across the length and breadth of the country do not want integrated schools, and that any attempt to force it on them might mean the loss of votes for Mr. Nixon in future elections.

Public opposition to busing has mounted in the U.S. In one southern town White parents were so incensed over the busing of Black pupils into their neighborhood that they turned over a bus carrying the children. I find it sad that hate could drive people to such extremes.

Excuses made to keep Blacks away from better-equipped and better-organized predominantly White schools are the same old familiar ones. One is talked about rather freely—that under the law it is illegal to send children to public schools outside their own neighborhood. The other excuse is given very quietly—that Blacks have not yet attained two disciplines which Whites demand of society—high intellect and proper behavior.

Grouping of Black and White students, we hear, tends to be a bad influence on the White kids. We see that in some integrated schools, especially in the South, large numbers of Black students are dismissed for infractions of discipline.

I agree totally that when groups of people are mixed, one may be a bad influence on the other, but I think it's about time that Whites woke up to the fact that their children are not all sanctified and that ours are not all accursed.

I experimented with marijuana and hashish. The

people who talked me into it were not Black. They were Whites from an exclusive suburban school who objected to my outright condemnation of drugs when I had never experimented with any hallucinogenics.

Two weeks after my talk the kids whose question about whether a drug problem in Ghana had led to my condemnation of drugs, visited me in my apartment. My eyes widened when they produced the marijuana, hashish and a pipe. They dared me. I coughed like a tubercular patient, but in five minutes I had been introduced to the drug culture. What makes Whites think that it is Blacks who will influence Whites, and not the other way around?

Practically every Washingtonian believes that the reason the city has a high crime rate is the widespread use of drugs by Blacks in the city. But drug usage is not limited to the inner cities. Drugs are used by both races. What people have been led to believe is that in Blacks, drugs lead to crime—but in Whites they lead to depression, alienation from families and in some rare instances suicide. All one needs to do is to read a Washington paper to get this impression.

In seven cases out of ten, the father of the inner city child cannot find a decent job. He lacks the education and the skill required for a good job. If he can find any job, the chances are that it is one he does not have his heart in. The salary is not enough to take care of himself, his wife, and the numerous children which he and his African cousins love to have. He considers himself a failure if he is unable to meet these responsibilities. The

American Black man often finds escape in one of two things—liquor or another woman with whom he has no children and who is less likely to nag him for his failure to provide for his family.

And when it comes to nagging the American Black woman is unbeatable. She is a victim of circumstances, too. She has been offered more in terms of education and jobs than the Black man. She has trouble finding a man of her color who matches her qualifications and status. Eventually, she has very little choice. She gets emotionally involved with someone who may not necessarily come up to her level, but since the desire of most women is to marry and raise a family, she temporarily accepts him for what he is.

No man likes to be made to feel inferior. The Black woman unconsciously makes her man feel inferior. She is better educated, has a better job.

I myself looked around for an American Black woman, or rather I waited for the day that a Black woman would hook me. Eventually, I had to play games with them because, as an African brought up to believe in male superiority, the dominance of Black women haunted me. I admired them for their beauty and great taste in clothes. They are articulate—but their aggressiveness can make a man feel castrated.

I am not amazed that there are more broken homes in Black America than in White America. The victims, however, are the children. They feel the strain of the quarrels, the drunkenness and the nagging. Outside their homes, the inner city children find nothing to brighten up their lives. All they see is squalor and depression.

If this is what the whole world is about, the child does not want to become a part of it. School has no meaning for him. He does not show any particular interest in what is being taught in school. His behavior finally presents a problem to the teachers.

I knew these problems of the inner city school child through my rounds of the schools. Some of the kids had warmed up to me and invited me to their homes to meet their parents. The father, in many instances, was never there. The Black woman was both a father and a mother to the children.

The problems of inner city kids never hit me as hard as the day I appeared at a corrections institution in Laurel, Maryland. The letter to my office asking the embassy to provide the speaker read: "The type of students we have here are the older, more aggressive, hard-core delinquents, who have been committed to the Welfare Department because of violations."

Throughout my lecture, I was cautious not to sound preachy or make any reference to crime. The young inmates' eagerness and response were so tremendous that I soon forgot their background. I relaxed. I enjoyed them as much as they enjoyed hearing someone talk of a country where there was no color hang-up, where they could walk freely wherever they wanted, where a Black man is the boss.

Then came a question I had not anticipated: "Do you believe in capital punishment?"

"Do you mean me or my government?"

"You," the whole room seemed to roar. I hesitated. All eyes were on me. "Yes," I said.

"Why?" they all shouted in unison. They were enjoying the game. I decided to go along with it.

"Why?" Because I think that no human being has a right to cut my life short. If anyone did, then the law must deal with him."

The reaction was spontaneous. Half the inmates had their hands up. Each one was demanding the floor. I pointed at one. He arose.

"Have you ever considered, Sir, why a boy like me might go to a grocery store and kill the grocer and take away his money? Have you ever considered why in spite of police and the fact that shopkeepers in our neighborhoods all have guns, we still do what we do?"

"Probably you need the money and you either can't get a job or don't want to work for practically zero."

Shouts drowned my voice.

"Okay, okay, you tell me then why you might do it," I said when their oh's and ah's had abated.

The confessions that those kids made were tragic. Some had killed for as little as fifty cents. Others had raped women anywhere between the ages of eight and eighty. And they did not impress me as being regretful for their actions and the retribution. They would do these things again if they had to start all over. Listening to them,

I came to realize that some of the kids stole or committed other crimes out of sheer material needs, and some just to prove they were "tough." But most of them committed crimes simply because the environment in which they lived bred the ugly habits they picked up. What struck me to the point of fright was their courage to meet force with force, if need be.

They were too young, I thought, to be so bold. When I told them this, they invited me to take leave from my job and move into the inner city for a week and see the relations existing between an inner city kid and the police. They were positive, they told me, that if I was able to survive it I would come out tough.

I did not need to accept their invitation to experience what they were talking about. I had seen the police in action in some Black neighborhoods. I had also seen altercations between the police and so-called hippie White youths. My own impression was that much of the trouble between the police and Blacks, between the police and White youths, could have been avoided if the bulk of the American police were more tactful and less corrupted by power.

My minister counsellor and I were on our way to Philadelphia one Sunday afternoon from New Castle, Delaware. This meant we either had to go by way of the Walt Whitman or the Benjamin Franklin Memorial Bridge.

The traffic, for a Sunday, was unusually light. As we came to the toll booth, we saw a bright yellow Camaro parked at the entrance of one of the two booths which were operating. On one side of the car stood a sad-looking Black girl. On the other side was a Black young man almost nailed to the side of the car, his hands stretched towards the heavens while a policeman searched him. What the cause of the arrest and search was we never found out.

The policeman moved toward the back of the car. Within seconds the young man shoved the girl into the car, and had taken off at tire-screeching high speed.

The officer drew his gun and fired three times. Each shot missed. He jumped into his own car and chased them firing all along. The incident shook my minister counsellor.

I had never heard gun shots other than those at ceremonial parades, nor had I ever seen anyone being fired at. The casual use of a gun sobered me.

I agree with reservations that in some cases the police have no alternative but to shoot. But I find it difficult to believe that with all of its technological development, the U.S. has failed to invent anything that could temporarily render a criminal powerless.

Two Ghanaian friends of mine came to see me one evening. I was late in returning home for our meeting so the boys sat outside the building for an hour waiting for me. While they were waiting, a policeman on a motor scooter came by, got off the scooter and walked aimlessly around them. Within ten minutes another one arrived. The two chatted quietly. My friends also sat there talking and waiting, unaware that they were the cause of police presence.

In another five minutes two more policemen arrived, this time in a car. After a brief meeting of the four officers, they approached my friends and asked them if they were looking for anything. I arrived just at that time. It was when I intervened that one of the officers explained that they had received twelve telephone calls from neighbors who complained there were two suspicious-looking Black boys hanging around the neighborhood.

Sometimes we are told that what we call discrimination is only a figment of our own imagination. But here we are dealing with a case of two Africans whose mere presence in a White neighborhood necessitated calls to the police.

The fact remains also that White prejudice against Blacks has reached the extent where the average Black man believes some of the things told about him by the White man. Even Blacks are distrustful of Black youths. Half of this distrust and fear is based on the fact that much of the crime in inner cities is committed by Blacks against Blacks. They do not do this out of hate for their fellow Black man. It only happens that the Black community is within easy reach of the criminally-inclined Black. I have seen elderly Blacks who pick on Black youths for any flimsy excuse.

Against this background of bad schools, bad police relations, poverty, lack of parental involvement, prejudice and depression, the Black child grows up not to be what he could be, but what society expects him to be.

The story does not end there. If he manages to graduate from high school, the Black youth, under pressure from his parents, may decide to continue his education. His parents tell him that if he is to obtain a job he must be twice as good as the White youth. Without a college education, he is told, his future is doomed. He agrees to go to college, but soon finds himself beset with two major problems: (1) The good American colleges and universities cost money. His parents cannot find the money to send him to the good schools. (2) Even if they are able to come up with the money, these colleges and universities will not admit him. His weak foundation in an ill-equipped predominantly Black school makes it hard for him to satisfy the standards set by these colleges.

Because of agitation and pressure from Black organizations, some top-level universities are now making a concerted effort to recruit Black students for their schools. Where the potential of the student indicates a measure of promise, he is apt to be awarded a scholarship. In some cases, these student-recruits have to spend their first year attending special remedial classes, in order that their level of education can be on par with that of their White colleagues and the small number of Black students whose backgrounds are comparable to that of the Whites.

The percentage of enrollment of Blacks in good universities is still low. Unless some drastic changes are made to upgrade the quality of inner city schools the problem will remain unsolved for a long time.

As we have seen, good colleges and universities are reluctant to enroll many of the Black high school graduates who wish to go to college. What do these Black students do? They turn their attention to the poor substitutes called Black colleges. My own pet reference to these colleges, founded and supported by federal or state governments or by religious sects, is "Witch, take this piece, so that you do not kill my child."

I come from a country that still believes in witchcraft. It is generally believed that in any gathering, one person is a witch. If there is a person at the gathering who is eating but who does not make any effort to share his food with the people around, the chances are that the witch will cast a spell on him. To avoid that he takes a little piece of his food and gives it away to anyone who wants it. This is precisely what the U.S. federal and state governments are doing with their college education for Blacks.

Some of these Black schools may be as good as some White ones, but this is still a doubtful matter. For one thing, running a university is an expensive venture. Each college or university wants to attract the best professors in the field. Those offering the best salaries recruit the best professors. The professors are interested not only in good salaries but also in an atmosphere where facilities for further research exist.

The Black colleges and universities lack both. The

type of dedication which will keep a Black professor in a Black university despite these lacks is fast disappearing. So we have a situation in which three-quarters of the Black world, including Africa and the Caribbean Islands, now has its most competent scholars on the faculties of predominantly White universities and colleges. Meanwhile, many instructors on the faculties of Black universities and colleges are qualified to teach only in high schools. They have no hope of ever being accepted by any well-known White university. These teachers are not all Black. There are many, many Whites, too.

Towards the latter part of 1970 two news items, published by papers in Washington and Baltimore, shed a little more light on the problems of Black colleges. The *Washington Evening Star* item said that publisher John Hay Whitney had willed fifteen million dollars to Yale University to finance the construction of six hundred residential units for students. The *Baltimore Sun,* in an article discussing the United Negro College Fund, said the organization had set itself the task of raising a hundred million dollars for its affiliated thirty-six Black colleges and universities. Reports later showed that U.N.C.F. grossed only seven million dollars—a mere drop in the academic ocean.

So Black institutions are financially and academically impoverished. The subsidies they receive from state and federal governments do not stretch far enough to upgrade teaching equipment, library books and other facilities. Black students take refuge in these institutions because the tuition fees are within their pockets. Their "pockets" of course, often depend on holding two jobs and studying simultaneously!

Recent reports indicate that the problem of money shortage is now facing even wealthy Ivy League schools. The administration itself is said to be cutting down drastically on its educational program to stop inflation. At a time when Blacks are making an effort to avail themselves of educational opportunities, low quality though it may be, they are told: "No money." Two of Washington's Black institutions, Federal City College and the Technical Institute, were unable to enroll many new students during 1970 because Congress did not appropriate enough funds. Federal City College alone had to turn down the applications of 2,500 prospective students.

The President of Miles College in Birmingham, Alabama, summed up the situation very sadly: "We just don't have enough money. We have never had enough money because there are very few people who see our roles in the destiny of this nation as important."

I was disturbed to see that in spite of the poor quality education in many Black colleges, more and more Blacks of college age felt that there was a paramount need for them to be educated in Black colleges. Some of that "need" I understood—the young men and women had no hope of being accepted by any name school since their educational ratings were so low. But I knew of cases where the students were brilliant but still insisted that they preferred Black schools, at least for their undergraduate work.

I had thought that one way in which our people could avail themselves of quality education and also help to break the myth that Blacks are intellectually inferior to Whites, was for the Blacks to fight tooth and nail to get into predominantly White institutions. I heard the arguments against this when I gave a small dinner party for an intelligent young friend of mine, Gary, who had been awarded a scholarship to Brown University in Rhode Island. Two other Black friends of mine, Lamar and Leon, showed some disappointment at the dinner when they learned that Gary was going to Brown and not to a Black college.

This came as a surprise to me—particularly since Leon and Lamar, both working on their doctorates, had received their first degrees from exclusive, predominantly White colleges. They argued that very few Blacks educated in White institutions identify with their own people. They lose their identity in White institutions, they think White and try to act White. They pass the same judgment on Blacks that Whites do. They consitute the Black middle class—the class that has been sitting on the fence too long, enjoying positions some of which were made possible by the agitation and rioting of the ordinary man in the street.

Did they have to tell me about the Black middle class and its attitudes? What I did not realize is that part of the indifference you find within the majority of the

Black middle class is due to attitudes shaped by their education in White institutions.

This attitude that leaves us halfway between Black and White, that make us appreciate White over Black, that has stifled progress and destroyed confidence in the Black man, has been recognized by some of our people. These people feel quite rightly that without a re-education of the Black mind, we would perpetually remain in cultural, economic and social slavery.

I was asked by several Whites, "Is it necessary to say 'Black is beautiful?' " Of course it is. The Black man has hated himself for too long. It's about time he became proud of what he is. To be proud of what he is, certain facts have got to be put at his disposal—he must learn the contributions that his own ancestors have made toward world civilization. This is what African Black Studies are all about.

But in this White-oriented and -dominated world, the call for such studies was given an entirely different interpretation. The general assumption was that Black students wanted degrees which did not require the use of the mental faculty!

The write-ups, discussions and arguments against African Black Studies did not impress me for a minute. I had heard these arguments before in a different context. In 1960 when the University College of Ghana became a full-fledged university, the Ghanaian government established an Institute of African Studies to offer long-neglected courses on Africa to the students. In addition to making the course compulsory to all undergraduates, the government also made the Institute a post-graduate school. The critics, this time in England, set to work crying that the Institute had been founded to promote hate against the former colonial powers. The critics did not say that a Ghanaian child spends all of his school life studying British and European history. They did not say that when Ghanaian kids watch "Tarzan" they enjoy seeing the White man "beat the hell out of that bad African tribal chief."

The Ghanaian students themselves were no less unkind in their criticisms of the Institute. The new Professor of African Studies was branded "Professor of Dondology" (Drums) and the "Professor of Indigenous Religions" became "Professor of Tigari" (a small religious sect). The students gave them these names to express their contempt at the introduction of these courses.

At Houston's prestigious Rice University, some friends sneaked me into a class where for a whole hour, I sat together with a hundred students or so listening to a lecture on the history of art. The course, I was later informed, was part of a four-year course leading to the award of a degree. In Austin, another friend of mine was studying for a degree in the history of furniture. Why, if people can study about such things as the history of art and furniture, can't they study about the history of their own people. Is it less important?

However, one aspect of the teaching of African Studies in America which I am not particularly happy about is the calibre of some of the people connected with its teaching. I heard them at various conferences, symposiums and lectures on Africa. My immediate reaction was negative. Their analyses of political developments in Africa only produced sneaky glances among the African diplomats present. At times I felt like jumping on my feet and shouting "Sir, you don't know a God damned thing about Africa. Either get your facts straight or quit mis-educating young minds."

Then there are the plethora of publications devoted entirely to commentary on Africa. I have had serious doubts about the competence of some of the people who write for these magazines. They seem to bow down to pressure from certain quarters, writing what some people want to hear.

Perhaps there is no easy answer to these problems and to make up for the many years of neglect. A good start would be truly equal financial funding for all school systems—Black and White.

White school children, in turn, should be taught some of the things I was learning. They might be as amazed as I was to learn how great a contribution Blacks have made to the economic base and cultural heritage of their country. And perhaps they might gain some insights into why people might want to tear down what they had built with their own hands.

8

If You Will Not Praise Me for My Contribution, Don't Spoil My Name

(Ghanaian Proverb)

In the course of my speaking engagements, I met Americans, young and old, Black and White, who could not visualize themselves living in any part of Africa. They theorized that "the widespread disease, poverty and the lack of modern technology" should make life in Africa pretty miserable. There were others who could not understand my eagerness to return home and leave behind all the comforts in America.

In Arlington, Virginia, one teacher in my audience of social science and African Studies teachers made such a big issue of American comfort and African misery that for once I thought I must break that diplomatic rule which maintains that a diplomat should always be complimentary to his host country. I told her that I had seen more misery in the U.S. than I had seen in any other country. That statement brought a sharp reaction from my audience.

I told my audience that if senseless and bizarre murders and assassinations made me, an outsider, bleed, what a great loss and misery it must be for the families involved. I told them I had reached a point in my life where listening to the news or reading the newspaper had become something to dread. The world has enough natural disasters. It does not need any more inflicted by man.

Without meaning to re-awaken the deep grief of the bereaved families, I mentioned the cases of actress Sharon Tate and her four friends; United Mine Workers' Jock Yablonski, his wife and his daughter; Dr. Ohta, his secretary and his family; and the countless other murders I read about whose motives were never clear. I did not see how human beings could be so intolerant of others that they would decide to settle quarrels at the muzzle of the gun or kill for a reason unspecified, and perhaps unknown, even to the killer.

At the peak of my annoyance and emotion, one woman, the only Black teacher in the room, remarked that I had not mentioned the name of any Black who had been so murdered in cold blood.

"Ma'am" I retorted, "the killing of Blacks in the U.S. happens with such consistency that it loses its newsworthiness. All you need to do is to pick up the paper or switch on your television. When it becomes public knowledge that more Black blood has been sacrificed by the police or by some individual, very little noise is made. Another commission of inquiry is appointed. What are their findings?

"If the killings were not motivated by the old hate and contempt for Blacks, the commission finds that the police over-reacted. So we are, in effect, like the snake in Ghanaian folklore.

"A farmer saw a snake on his farm. Some of his yams were missing so he concluded that only the snake could have eaten them. Immediately he killed the snake, whereupon the snake rolled over, and with its stomach to the world proved that the stomach was empty. It had eaten nothing that called for such a fate. But the damage was already done."

At that moment, I could not have cared less whether someone from the State Department or the C.I.A. was present, or whether anyone in my audience would quote what a diplomat had said about his host country. I was making public a feeling which I had privately made known to some of my close White friends. It was about time, I felt, that Whites tried to see how things looked from our vantage point.

What had really so infuriated me was that I had privately discussed the issue of violence in America with some of my closest friends. Many of them, I discovered, did not share my grave fear that unless great efforts were made to stamp out violence, America was in serious trouble. They shrugged their shoulders and informed me that violence was nothing new to the American way of life. America, they declared, was born in violence.

But although they made that statement, each time that Blacks rioted and burned their neighborhood, some of these same friends would ask in a discussion: "What do the Negroes hope to achieve through violence?" I am divided as to who loses each time a Black neighborhood is burned down, although the consensus among Whites and middle-class Black Americans is that it is the Blacks themselves who become the losers.

On my first visit to Watts, in Los Angeles, I could not believe I was actually there. I pleaded with the friend I was with, a White, to drive me to the real Watts and stop giving me a window-dressing job. For more than two hours, Richard drove me into Watts, around Watts and inside Watts. "What the hell did these people here riot for?" I asked. "If those of us on the East Coast could have anything half as decent, we would keep our mouths shut."

Richard's brother, a poverty worker, later answered that question for me. "All that glitters isn't gold, Fred. Don't be fooled by the good appearance of Watts. I am White, but I know that the jobs are just not available for the people there. There are many reasons why the people of Watts did what they did."

I kept my mouth shut. Being Black did not mean I had all the answers. Besides as the Ghanaians say, "It is the one who lies close to the fire who knows what effect the fire has on his skin." The people of Watts knew better than I did. The people in any Black neighborhood know what the conditions are. I saw it, but after seeing it, what? I left to go and sleep in a White neighborhood. This is why in spite of my frowning on Blacks who start the riots, I cannot pass judgment.

I chose not to discuss the plight of Black people with even the closest of my White friends. This type of discussion invariably left me temporarily suspicious of their sincerity. It was distressing to discover that there were very few Whites even among the young and the educated who saw our plight from its right perspective. The majority seemed unconcerned.

Occasionally, you meet Whites who show a genuine concern for Blacks. They throw a few leads which uplift your soul. You are fooled. You enter into a serious discussion. Suddenly, it dawns on you that the two of you are looking at the problem with two different sets of eyes. There always seems to be a certain amount of fear of Blacks by Whites. Some can not clearly define what these fears are and upon what grounds they are founded. Economics and fear of violence seem to play a leading role in this White fear of Blacks.

Moans, groans and tears have become a part of our existence ever since that ill-fated day we came into contact with Whites. World opinion, formed by the media, has little sympathy for our moans, our groans and our tears.

This happened in Ghana in 1948: Ghanaian soldiers who had fought for the British government during World War II marched towards the residence of the-then British

Governor to demand jobs. As they approached, the White police commissioner ordered his troops to shoot. Immediately four of them fell.

And in Sharpeville, South Africa, seventy-two Africans who had refused to carry identity cards were struck to the ground, for no other reason.

Rhodesia illegally declared its independence. A handful of Whites became rulers of millions of Africans. Britain refused to intervene militarily. But when tiny Black Anguilla took the same action, Britain retook the island militarily in no time.

Before Kent State there was Orangeburg State in South Carolina. How many remember? If Kent State had not preceded Mississippi State, that incident would have been forgotten.

Nothing worried me as much as walking through Black neighborhoods and seeing strong, healthy Black men, standing in front of bars and liquor shops and telling jokes. After a while, I began to think that perhaps these men were as lazy as I had heard. It was difficult for me to understand why these men would stand on street corners idle when they had themselves and their families to support.

I discussed this matter in depth with Blacks and Whites alike. I wanted as many varying views as I could get from the Blacks who did not work and the Whites who could "not find qualified Negroes to fill responsible positions." It was at that time that I saw Anne Moody, author of *Coming of Age in Mississippi,* on television.

Of the books I have read on the racial situation in America, none moved me as deeply as hers. In one paragraph the story is told of a Black woman, Emma, lying in her hospital bed with a leg injury. Emma had been shot at by her brother-in-law while she was trying to stop a fight between him and her sister. Her family is naturally enraged over the shooting. But Emma, in pain, says to the family, "It ain't Wilbert's fault. Him and Janie wouldn't be fightin' if Wilbert could get a job and make enough money to take care of them children. If these damn White folks ain't shootin' Niggers' brains out they are starvin' them to death. A Nigger can't make it no way he try in this f . . n' place."

The bitter truth hit me that it was very easy for me and other people to assume that the jobs were available and that the Blacks did not want them. The crux of the matter was that the jobs were unavailable. Where they were, Blacks did not possess the skills specified for the jobs, and even if they possessed the skills they would have to be twice as qualified before they could get them.

Sometimes they have to struggle with the unions, some of which are so biased that they will not accept Blacks for membership. Without union backing, the chances of a job are almost nil.

After a while, I had to ask myself, "Well, since when did the Black man become lazy? Is he really lazy or it is the society he lives in that has reduced him to a beggar?" Blacks, it appeared to me then, were being accused of laziness not because they were lazy but because their cheap labor on tobacco and cotton fields and in many varied construction jobs, which have all helped to make the U.S. what it is today, has outlived its usefulness in this age of technology.

Evidence of this can be found in the "Journal of Commissioners for Trade and Plantation" (pp. 254-255), recorded in 1726 and kept at the Public Record Office in Britain:

Mr. Splatt: Mr. Splatt likewise sworn, acquainted their lordships, that he was lately come from Carolina, and that the Province was then very well supplied with negroes. That he never knew of any negroes brought into that country by the Company, excepting those contracted for with Mr. Wragg. That the Province annually takes about 1,000 per annum, and that they sell at about L30 or L35 sterling per head. That a negro can make F10 per annum clear profit to his master, and that he thinks the Colonies would be cheaper and better supplied by the separate traders than the Company.

Mr. Perry: Mr. Perry, a Virginia merchant, being sworn, acquainted their lordships, that by his accounts, that province is very plentifully supplied with negroes, and that there has been but very few of the Company's ships at Virginia since he has been concerned in trade, which is about three or four years.

Mr. Bradley: Mr. Bradley being sworn, acquainted their lordships, he has been in the trade to Virginia above 20 years, and that the Province has been well supplied with negroes by the separate traders. That the labour of a negro produces about L15 annual duty to the Crown. That he believes negroes are cheaper now than they were formerly, but admits that there was formerly a duty of 5 per cent, laid on negroes, which made them dearer.

Mr. Hunt: Mr. Hunt, a trader to Maryland, being sworn, acquainted their lordships, that of late years there are annually imported into Maryland between 500 and 1,000 negroes. That the produce of a negro is about 4 hogsheads of tobacco per annum, and that the duty of 4 hogsheads is about L40 or L50. That the Province would take off more negroes, if they could get them, and that they would increase their trade. That Gambia, the Northern coast, and Angola, are the chief parts of Africa from whence Maryland is supplied. That he believes, if the trade was confined to a Company, negroes would be dearer, and the Province worse supplied. That the price of negroes had formerly been L30 or L40, but are now sold at L18, L20 and L25.

Mr. Byam: Mr. Byam, a trader to Antigua, being sworn, acquainted their lordships, that he has traded to that island about twelve years, and that during that time the island has been well supplied with negroes by the separate traders. That without them they could not make their produce of sugar, cotton, ginger, etc. That there was made 19,000 hogsheads of sugar in that island last year. That negroes have been bought thither so plentifully by the separate traders that they have been forced to carry some away unsold. That they pay less sugar for negroes now than they did formerly, and that he apprehends the Plantations would be in a very bad condition, if the trade of Africa were restrained to a company.

Mr. Gerrish: Mr. Gerrish being sworn, acquainted their lordships, that he had lived at Montserrat many years. That the island had been supplied with negroes, 3 to 1 better since the duty of 10 per cent ceased than before. That they had as many brought by the separate traders as the planters could pay for, and that they never had the like supplies from the company. That the planters sometimes sent ships themselves to Africa for slaves. That during the duty of 10 per cent they made about 2,000 but now they make 3,000 hogsheads of sugar annually, and that a less quantity of sugar is now paid for negroes than formerly.

We see from this document that the sweat and labor of the Black man have contributed greatly to America's present prosperity.

All around the world there are very few Whites who realize or would acknowledge the contributions that Africans and people of African descent have made toward the development of their economies. Britain, France, and Portugal, the biggest colonials, did not colonize Africa just to bring "civilization," religion or culture to the people. They were motivated by what they could get out of colonialism.

At the time of the second World War, I was in grade school. I and all the other children in school in Ghana were told to contribute certain quotas of cracked palm-kernels. Failure to provide your apportioned quota resulted in heavy caning. We spent all of our weekends hunting for palm kernels, cracking them with stones, and hurting our fingers. We dreaded school on Monday since we did not know whether what we had was enough or not. Little did we know then that these kernels were badly needed in British factories to substitute for certain materials that had become unavailable during the war.

+   +   +

I was in America when the "Philadelphia Plan" became law. Under this plan, Blacks were assured of a certain percentage of the labor on every construction job involving federal contracts and funds. To the best of my recollections, the most violent response to the plan and other related ones came from northern construction workers. I had to fight back the tears welling in my eyes as I sat in my apartment, watching on television a helpless Black youth being clubbed by a White construction worker in Olympia, Washington. He had been hired under the plan as an apprentice worker, but in the violent demonstration against the plan, the youth became one of the victims. White construction workers feared that hiring and training of jobs for construction would ultimately lead to their replacement by Blacks.

It is these same White construction workers who make the most bitter remarks about deductions made from their salaries to look after welfare recipients. One would think that the only way White construction workers could show they wanted Blacks off the welfare rolls would be by agreeing to the plan to hire them.

From time to time we hear or read of gains that Blacks have made since Reconstruction. The thing about these press reports is that the headline usually gives you hope, but as you read on you find that the picture is not quite as rosy as the heading made it seem.

According to the Director of the Office of Equal Opportunity in Washington, D.C., James Baldwin, "In spite of overall gains, Negroes continue to be grossly underrepresented in the upper grades of all pay systems. On June 30, 1969, for example, Negroes comprised less than 25 percent of General Schedule employees above GS-12" ($14,192 yearly). Other figures quoted by Mr. Baldwin were as follows: (1) 44 percent of Black men were employed under the wage board system which covers mostly menial jobs. Their average salary is $6,419. (2) Blacks represent 77.5 percent of the school system; 74.4 percent of the Welfare Department; 72 percent of the public

Health Department; 43.5 percent of the Highway Department; 35 percent of the police force; 30.4 percent of the Correction Department; and 19.2 percent of the Fire Department. These figures are all for the District of Columbia, which is about 70 percent Black.

On July 5, 1970, the *New York Times* also reported that the federal census data indicated a widening gap between incomes of Black and White families. Incomes for Blacks went up 7.6 percent from 1959 to 1958, but those of Whites rose 15.6 percent. Within New York City, the proportion of poor Black families—those with incomes under $4,000—stayed at about 31 percent.

These figures indicate that after four hundred years, the American Black man still has far to go to make significant headway into the economic mainstream of his country. Far too many Whites sincerely believe that the American Black man should wait for progress to come gradually. He should not demand it now.

The Urban League sponsored a survey on public reaction to Black gains. It must have been shocked when the results revealed that 42 percent of the Whites interviewed by Louis Harris (1) thought that Blacks are pushing too fast for equality, and (2) disapproved of the U.S. Supreme Court's 1954 school desegregation decision, and favored separate schools for Blacks and Whites.

I think that anyone who makes the argument that Blacks are pushing too fast overlooks an important factor. What guarantees, if any, does Black America have that the U.S. will continue its present economic prosperity and military strength? We have all seen in history that no one particular country has continuously enjoyed economic and political dominance over the rest of the world. These things recycle.

Should it ever happen that the U.S. becomes a third or fourth or even a tenth-rate power, what gains then would the Black man have made in America? He would have suffered in vain. I see such a possibility coming already.

I soon began to wonder if the only way Blacks can improve their status in the U.S. is by building political power, and whether Black America could learn any lessons in this from Black Africa.

9

The Will of the People Is Greater Than The Man's Machinery

(Huey Newton,
Black Panther Leader)

In early 1970, Mayor Walter Washington of the District of Columbia, accompanied by his wife, Bennetta, visited a number of European countries. In Paris, Mrs. Washington met with the wives of American personnel in the city.

The *Washington Daily News* quoted Mrs. Washington as telling the wives that discontent leads to progress. She is reported to have said:

"I have a great feeling for young people. I think they are marvelous. They are discontented and the only time you move ahead is when you are discontented. If you are content, you sit and get fat and nothing happens."

Before this statement came to my attention, I had learned that Bennetta Washington's outspokenness had won her a place in the hearts of the African diplomatic circles. Mrs. Washington, I was informed, was sharp and to the point without mincing any words.

Ever since the publication of her Paris statement, I have done much thinking and re-thinking about it. It has helped me to analyze the political and economic developments which have taken place in Africa since the wind of change swept through the continent in the late fifties. It is an appraisal I had never made before.

Before my arrival in the U.S. it had never occurred to me that one could identify some of the problems of the African nations with some of the problems facing Black Americans. Three and a half years have now taught me that (1) the economies of the African nations are so hopelessly controlled by the Western nations that it makes a mockery of political independence; (2) that while the African nations have their hands stretched out to the Western nations for "Trade not aid," the Black Americans are also saying to White America "Jobs not welfare."

The problem in Africa is, however, more acute than that of Black America. Black America is discontent. They agitate. They riot. They holler. Gradually they are moving ahead. White America sees that it can no longer ignore a minority which it has enslaved, maltreated and ignored. The average African is content. He sits and gets fat and nothing happens. If he fails to get a job, if taxes are on the increase, if consumer goods are unavailable, he knows who to hold responsible. That "who" is his government, not the Western nation which controls his country's economy to such an extent that the government cannot keep most of the election pledges it made to the people.

A classic example of the situation I am referring to exists in my own country, Ghana. In 1969 the Ghana Army and police who had seized power three and a half years ago, formally announced that it was lifting the ban on political activities. A new constitution had been written. Elections would be held in August. Prior to this announcement, it had become an open secret that Ghana's external debts before the Army took over totalled almost a billion dollars. The country was spending 25 percent of its total earnings to service that debt on the basis of the agreements which the Nkrumah Government had signed. The growth rate of the economy was less than one percent per annum. The population growth was about 2.6 percent. Out of a total labor force of 2.4 million, 600,000 were out of work.

The conditions in the country were so grim that I could not understand the zeal of the nine Ghanaians who emerged as leaders of the various political parties formed to contest the elections. I knew my own people and how they reacted to different situations. They were looking for miracles. They were looking for a leader who could stop inflation overnight, provide jobs for all and make life a little more comfortable for them. I knew that they would be in such haste for reforms that they would expect the impossible from whoever they elected as leader. The fact that the country had managed to survive economically by suppressing and postponing its balance of payment problems for ten years was of little or no concern to the large majority of Ghanaians. The fact that the Western nations were pressing Ghana hard for repayment of old debts did not bother the minds of the average Ghanaian.

In the election of August, 1969, Dr. Busia's Progress party won a landslide victory. It won 105 of the 144 seats contested. The Ghanaians had thrown their full support behind Dr. Busia who for several years had been a strong opponent of Dr. Nkrumah. Dr. Busia had warned Ghanaians about the corrupt and dictatorial government of Dr. Nkrumah, and had asked them to cease giving any more support. Once the Ghanaians had clearly evidenced what Dr. Busia warned them against, they decided to give Dr. Busia a chance.

I felt extremely sorry for Dr. Busia the day he was sworn in with great pomp and fanfare as Prime Minister of Ghana. I was least impressed by the cheers and rejoicing of the people. All of it reminded me of the old adage of people who said, "Hosannah saying crucify him." The economic problems were so immense that I could not see how Dr. Busia could perform the great miracle that his people were expecting from him. I knew that the time was not far behind when the Ghanaians would be disenchanted with Busia's administration. He could not correct the economic problems without introducing some hardships on the people. The Ghanaians were ready for anything but hardships even if such hardships were only momentary.

Dr. Busia made no bones about being pro-West. We

all thought that the Western nations would be gratified by Dr. Busia's leaning towards them and his desire to build a strong democratic machinery in Ghana to write off some of the debts that his government was not responsible for or reschedule them in such a way that the country would have a break. To put it in Ghanaian parlance the debtors "sat on Ghana's balls" to such an extent that the poor man had to tackle the problem from the roots. The hardships that the Ghanaians least wanted had to be introduced. Under advice from certain world financial bodies his government devalued the currency by forty-four percent. That was the straw that broke the camel's back.

At three o'clock on the morning of 13th January, 1972 I was awakened from my sleep by the telephone. Normally, I do not answer my phone after nine in the evening, but I had gone to bed the night before with such premonition and uneasiness that I decided to answer that time. My hands shook vigorously as I lifted the receiver. A reporter of a reputable news agency, assuming that I already had wind of a military take-over in Ghana, asked if there had been any further developments since the first announcement. I told him "No." The ambassador had gone to Ghana for his father's funeral. I was lost in confusion when the phone rang again. This time it was the minister counsellor, the number two man. He had received two calls from Ghanaians in the U.S. informing him of the coup. Could I check the veracity of the news? I called Associated Press. They confirmed it.

Calmly, I conveyed the news to the minister counsellor. I broke down immediately. My whole world seemed to be coming to an end. I knew that whoever had initiated the coup was motivated by his strong concern for the economic suffering of the Ghanaians, but was the coup an answer to our problem? I could visualize the Ghanaians rejoicing over the news of the take-over, but I wondered whether they could see that beyond the coup there was anything more than political and economic instability. It was going to be extremely difficult to attract the foreign investment that the Ghanaians needed very badly. I also saw that even though the Western nations did very little to bail Dr. Busia out of his country's economic plight, they were so annoyed at his overthrow that without putting in so many words they were determined to punish the Ghanaians by dragging their feet about aid. I saw Ghana reverting to a situation which existed in the early sixties in which the Government absorbed practically eighty percent of the working force because there were virtually no private concerns. On the face of it there was employment but production was low, and the cost to the government so astronomical that the coffers were becoming exhausted.

For the first time in my life I lost faith in my own people. I seriously toyed with the idea of renouncing my citizenship and leaving the Ghanaians to please themselves. On second thought I realized that no matter what I do and say I am a Ghanaian, first and foremost. I belong there. I have a responsibility toward the country, and I cannot isolate myself from its problems. Whoever says that one cannot be sentimental about a country is wrong.

What Africans need is an awareness that most of their problems go far beyond their governments.

Throughout their histories, African nations have been reduced to mere producers of raw materials. Ghana, for instance, has always enjoyed the reputation of being the world's largest producer of cocoa. Ghana, Nigeria, Ivory Coast, Togo and Cameroon have jointly produced more than half of the world's cocoa. The only country in the Western hemisphere which grows cocoa is Brazil.

And yet until independence not one single of these cocoa-producing countries in Africa had a chocolate factory! All the cocoa was exported to foreign countries. The cocoa beans came back to Ghanaians in the form of chocolate. The average Ghanaian could not even afford a bar of chocolate. It was a luxury.

Ghana alone produces 300,000 tons of cocoa annually. The crop is the country's life blood. It is the country's biggest foreign exchange earner. Without it the country's economic survival is shaky. Yet the price of cocoa like so many other produce of the African nations have fluctuated so much so that the African governments have great difficulties budgeting.

This was what Dr. Busia had in mind when in an address to the New York Cocoa Exchange in the spring of 1970, he said:

> I do know that some people here depend upon the instability of the cocoa market for their very livelihood. You will appreciate that we, with our whole

national destiny bound up with this cocoa industry, need stability. We need to be able to develop our country and that means relying on what we have, upon cocoa which is our most important product. To be able to do this, we need a stable market and remunerative prices for our cocoa.

You all know that we have been engaged in negotiations for an International Cocoa Agreement for more than a decade. Let me be frank and say that it is my understanding that your organization, the New York Cocoa Exchange, is one of the most intransigent sources of opposition to an International Cocoa Agreement that would be an important instrument for our national development and our economic security. What I would ask you is to try to adopt a positive approach towards this matter on the basis that it is an important interest of your poorer partners in this cocoa business. I want you to examine frankly with us the extent to which supporting us in an International Agreement would be to the detriment of your own interests as an organized commodity market and as individuals who make your living out of this market.

The *New York Times* in an article published on November 30, 1969, said that Ghana lost $60,000,000 worth of much-needed foreign exchange in 1968 because of what it called "the cocoa spies." "These spy-men paid by foreign companies to predict the size of Ghana's cocoa crop out-guessed the country's State Company and were able to win a fat profit for their employers," the paper said.

The article also pointed out that the spies move all over the country to gather information for their estimates, which they send to companies dealing in consignments of cocoa sold for delivery several months later.

The Ghanaians want to see a reduction in food prices. They want to see a plentiful supply of consumer goods. Above all, taxes should be reduced. But how does the government satisfy these demands when cocoa prices upon which it places most of its hopes are never improving? How does the government fulfill its election pledges when it uses twenty-five percent of its foreign exchange servicing bad debts which our so-called friends encouraged us to incur? At the time of Ghana's second coup cocoa prices had fallen by fifty percent. The cry for better health facilities, more schools for a growing population, improved communications, housing and water persisted.

When I was a child my father, like many fathers over the world, opened a small savings account for me. But in addition to the savings, he gave me an education. Today, that savings is all used up—but I am making a living out of my education.

Independence has brought great responsibility to bear on the African leaders. The leaders see that great misery abounds everywhere. Masses of people have not had any education; medical facilities are few and far between; communications between villages do not exist.

So what do the African leaders do? They fall on the savings bequeathed to them at the time of independence to develop the infrastructure. By the time they are halfway through with the first stage of development, a great proportion of the savings is used up. Unlike you and me, these countries had no education that they could depend on. They only had savings. Now even that is gone and there is still a great deal to be done.

Britain left Ghana at the time of independence with a total saving of $500,000,000. I will be the first person to admit that part of the dwindled savings could be blamed on gross economic mismanagement of the First Republic, but some of it also had to be spent on projects which the British had badly neglected and which the people needed.

I am personally of the opinion that part of the African's lack of awareness of problems of development is the fault of the respective African governments.

A large segment of educated Africans see themselves as politically aware. They probably are if all it takes to be politically aware is to become a member of a political party and to help a party to win votes. To me more is required, the ability of the African to place the problem where it lies. Unfortunately the most educated and sophisticated Africans are the ones who do not seem to be aware of the problems. They are sometimes the African governments' worst enemy. I personally think that at the time of independence the African governments should have educated the masses on the problems of the state. I know that in Ghana, for instance, the reaction of the people to such a campaign would have been: "Ah, they told us so. The Black man is incapable of self-rule. 'Buronyi ara nye John.' The government is trying to find a scapegoat." But in a country where people thrive on rumors such a campaign could not be ignored.

Political education will not produce sympathy from the people if the governments themselves do not cut unnecessary expenditure and prove to the people that they are sincere, honest men, dedicated to the service of their country.

That lack of political awareness among Africans is also prevalent among Black Americans. More and more young Blacks take great pride in asserting their political awareness, but I have seen something that they do not seem to see. I was visiting Detroit, Michigan at the time of the 1969 mayoral election. Two candidates, including Dennis Austin, a Black man, were the strong favorites. After a tour of the city of Detroit, I could not understand why anybody, Black or White, would want to become the mayor of such a beat-up city. Like many of the northern cities I visited, Detroit was sorry-looking. To me, anybody who won the election and became mayor was not to be envied. The problems were immense.

To rebuild any of the major northern cities and come to grips with their social problems, a mayor, Black or White, needs an economic miracle. If Whites moved from the city at a time when a White was in City Hall, what makes Blacks think that the rest will stay on when a Black man becomes mayor? There are Whites who flee the cit-

214

ies out of prejudice. Others take such a course out of fear that there might be a breakdown of law and order once a Black man is elected mayor. So we have on our hands a situation where the Whites leave and take away with them their taxes and loyalty. Big businesses seem to follow the trend.

What I found ludicrous were the number of my Black middle-class friends who lent their support and time organizing Blacks in the city to vote for a Black mayor. These friends invariably live outside the cities and pay their taxes to a suburban administration. But they help a Black man to become elected in the city. What funds will he work with?

Recent statistics show that almost all of the major northern cities have either become predominantly Black or are on the verge of becoming so. The great majority of these Blacks are poor and unskilled. They have migrated into the cities looking for employment. If they are not on welfare, God only knows how some of them make a living. They have no properties that can be taxed. Rather the city has to support them. Why then do we Blacks put so much time and energy into campaigning and voting for Black men to become big-city mayors at a time when the U.S. is becoming more and more suburbanized?

Some Blacks, including knowledgeable ones, call the election of Black mayors "political power." I do not see it. If these mayors have any power, it is the power to boost the confidence of the Black man. Nothing more.

Black mayors do not only have on their hands the

problems of finding money for their programs. They have also to contend with local, state and sometimes a national administration which does not take too kindly to open flirtation with a Black administration. A mayor cannot be successful without the cooperation of these administrations. Charles Evers, Carl Stokes, Kenneth Gibson, Richard Hatcher and Walter Washington must have realized by now that occupying City Hall is one thing and keeping the faith of the people who put them there is another. Why has Carl Stokes stepped down?

These mayors sincerely believe at the time of their election that they can revive the cities. Once in the mayoral chair they learn that getting elected is one thing. Solving the problems is another. The Black man also expects miracles from his new Black mayor. He turns against him when he sees that the mayor has not lived up to his election pledge. He is disappointed. As a result I heard in Black America the same words I had heard in Africa: "Put the White man there." Whites may have expressed some dissatisfaction with previous White mayors, but once a Black mayor fails, color sets in. It becomes "I told you so."

Every time a Black candidate was involved in an election, I sat up all night to follow television results of the election. But after the Black had been declared a winner, I asked myself "Now what?" Until such time that American Blacks can be a political force, no amount of senators, congressmen and mayors will help. Without a strong backing, White America can always ignore Black leaders and their people. It is this strong political force that I looked for but never found in Black America.

Blacks would be submerged in any alliance with Whites. They would be used to build the political ambition of some. In the final analysis, only a few Blacks would benefit from such an alliance.

Personally, I do not subscribe to the view that President Nixon is anti-Black. He told his first press conference that he had learned from Robert Finch that Blacks did not consider him a friend, and promised that by his actions the Blacks would eventually change their views about him. Whether after three years in the White House he has helped the Blacks to change their views remains to be seen. One thing, however, is clear. President Nixon is a shrewd politician who knows where the votes are and what the wishes of the voters are.

Political education and organization is as badly needed in Black America as it is in Africa. I would like to see a more personal relationship existing between African ambassadors and the Black caucus. We can use and help each other. It should not stop at cocktail parties and dinners. It should be taken a step further—between American Black and African leaders.

Very little of such a relationship has existed so far for two basic reasons. One is that some of the African leaders have been intimidated into believing that any open flirtation with Black leaders might offend the U.S. government and result in a cut or denial of aid.

A segment of the Black student population has also

continued to sow seeds of discord between U.S. Blacks and Africans. I have sometimes wondered whether these students realize that certain statements that they make which are quoted for publication sour relations between our peoples, or whether they are intended to strengthen relations. They see themselves as the standard-bearers of a united Black world. They even arrogate to themselves the right to decide who should rule which African country.

As a Ghanaian living in the U.S. I can understand and appreciate the high esteem in which the average Black American holds Ghana's ex-President, Nkrumah. He organized and led his people to become the first Black nation to achieve its independence. He sought to make Africans aware that without unity there was little that they could achieve individually. He embarked on a project to unite Africa politically. Nkrumah came out strongly against colonialism and neo-colonialism. He worked towards Black emancipation and dignity. He developed Ghana's manpower and infrastructure.

But like many leaders who start out well, he let power go to his head. In defiance of African traditions that "the road builder does not see that that portion behind him is not straight and needs an observer to draw his attention to it," Nkrumah wiped away all traces of opposition. He became despotic and imprisoned people senselessly. While he asked his people to make sacrifices, he allowed his own party hierarchy to become a new undisciplined upper class.

The people cheered, but they were hungry. Taxes had been increased. Food prices had gone up. Parents were afraid to criticize the government in front of their children, who had been mobilized by the party. Wives were being taken away from their husbands. If the man complained, whoever was responsible for taking the wife framed up a story and accused the man of subversive activities. Before the husband knew what was happening he was in detention. It was an age of fear and general madness.

On the 24th of February, 1966, the Ghana Army, like a bolt out of the blue, came to the rescue. It was a day that the Ghanaians had longed for and prayed for. We took to the streets. We drummed, danced, and somersaulted, and in traditional fashion thanked the gods for their help.

The new government mounted an extensive campaign outside Ghana to explain the necessity for the change in government. There were some Ghanaians who questioned the government's motives. As far as most people were concerned, Nkrumah had been deposed. If there were any people who wanted him, they could have him on a silver platter.

Certain Black militants and students credited the Central Intelligence Agency with the planning and the execution of Nkrumah's overthrow. No amount of explanation has or ever will change their reasoning. I have reached a point where I ignore completely this faction of

Black militants and students who stubbornly insist that the C.I.A. overthrew Nkrumah.

All through history we have had instances where the people's revolution has overpowered the arms of government. If the people of Ghana had loved Nkrumah as much as these militants want the world to believe, the events of February 24, 1966 would have been short-lived. Nkrumah would still be in power.

The overthrow of President Obote of Uganda brought the same reaction from outside Black militants. How can they live three thousand or more miles away and jump to the amazing conclusion that the people love their leaders, but that because the leaders come out so strongly against imperialism, colonialism and neo-colonialism, the Western powers bring about their downfall?

If these militants persist in glorifying that baseless allegation that the C.I.A. overthrew Nkrumah, it is only fair also to glorify the following rumors: (1) That Nkruman planned the late Saturday night assassination of the former President of Togo, Sylvannus Olympio. Olympio was strongly opposed to Nkrumah's ambition to join his country to Ghana. (2) That Nkrumah had a responsibility in the cold-blooded assassination of Alhaji Sir Abubakar Tafawa Balewa, Prime Minister of Nigeria, Alhaji Ahmadu Bello, Prime Minister of the-then Northern Nigeria and Chief Akintola, Prime Minister of the-then Western Nigeria. These men were all very cool to Nkrumah's idea of an African continental government. After the assassinations had been announced, Nkrumah committed a grievous, un-African mistake. He paid a very sarcastic tribute to Sir Abubakar on a brilliantly sunny day. The sarcasm and the famous words "Sir Abubakar died of circumstances he did not understand," confirmed the deep suspicion of many Ghanaians that Nkrumah had a hand in the assassinations. (3) That the several African leaders who accused Nkrumah of subversive activities against their states were not paranoid. We cannot be moral about one and dismiss another as unfounded.

I am not, by any stretch of the imagination, underestimating the power of the C.I.A. or absolving it of its involvement in international politics, but one must also not be paranoid about the agency.

All I am saying is that in spite of wild allegations of C.I.A. involvement in the Ghana coup, no one has as yet come up with any substantial evidence other than the wicked, baseless one that the-then U.S. Ambassador to Ghana, Franklyn Williams, a Black man and a personal friend of Nkrumah, served as an intermediary between the Ghana Army and the C.I.A. The situation is best explained in terms of a Ghanaian proverb: "If you smell, people give off bad air in your presence and blame you for it." The C.I.A.'s own reputation has made it susceptible to accusations. It is not responsible for all African political changes.

I never met Dr. Martin Luther King in person. He was assassinated three months before my arrival in the U.S. I admired him. I thought he was a great leader, although my accounts of him were based on newspaper and radio reports.

Since my arrival in the U.S. I have had the opportunity to discuss the former leader with a cross-section of the Black community. A few elderly Blacks and many, many young Blacks regard Dr. King as the epitome of the White man's Negro leader. They do not see the good that I saw in him. I keep away from that discussion now, because they know the man much better than I do. What makes Black militants and some Black students assume that they knew Nkrumah and the Ghana situation better than the Ghanaians?

Stokely Carmichael says that his greatest objective is to organize Ghanaians to revolt against their constitutionally-elected government, return Nkrumah to power and use Ghana as a base for war against White injustice. Mr. Carmichael is an emotional man. He is not very circumspect. If he were he would have learned by now that his statements definitely make the African leaders suspicious of all young Blacks.

Anytime you threaten a government you put that government on the alert. A case in point was the May Day Tribes' threat to close down the U.S. federal government in 1971. Washington looked like a battleground on May 1. A government will protect itself. So because of Mr. Carmichael and his followers, African embassies become suspicious anytime a young Black applies for a visa to visit the motherland. Every young Black is seen as a potential saboteur. If we are not careful we will find oursleves in a situation where very few Blacks will have the opportunity to travel to Africa and to experience that feeling which many Blacks returning from Ghana recounted to me in my office.

At this point, I must express deep concern about an element in the struggle of Africans and peoples of African descent. It seems to me that rather than getting to the roots of our own mistakes and shortcomings we are beginning to find excuses for them. No one can deny that injustices against us still exist; that we have been oppressed for too long; that as a result of our colonial and slave experience many of us don't know where we belong, but let us be honorable enough to accept our own failings. A struggle becomes stagnant once the people involved engage in rhetoric instead of action. I wish to see more constructive criticisms in the struggle.

I do not, for instance, see the justification for Ghana's dependence on the U.S. Peace Corps for teachers in the liberal arts field. We do it simply because our own college graduates do not think that to be of service in villages to their own people is a worthwhile sacrifice. But at the same time these young Ghanaians accuse the government of harboring C.I.A. agents—the Peace Corps volunteers.

In July 1970 the new British Conservative government announced that it would revoke the UN Security Council ban on arms shipment to South Africa. Many of the African countries within the Commonwealth clearly stated that they would oppose any move by the British government to take such an action, which would mean arming that apartheid government to the teeth. Prior to the British announcement it had been an open secret that the U.S., Canada, France, West Germany, Japan, Italy and Belgium had all violated the UN resolution and had unabashedly supplied South Africa with arms.

Nigeria, Tanzania and Zambia threatened that if Britain went ahead with its plan, they would pull out of the Commonwealth. Then came the Ghana government statement which called on Britain to suspend its decision until it had due consultation with other Commonwealth states.

It became my responsibility to circulate the Ghanaian government statement to Ghanaian students in the U.S. Compared to what Nigeria, Tanzania and Zambia had said, the Ghana statement was weak. Ghana was taking a back-seat position, and the students who received the press release harrassed me in person and on the phone about our stand.

What I did not have the courage to tell the students was that even though the Ghana statement was mild, it was perhaps the most realistic of all. A break, or pulling out of the Commonwealth? Who are the biggest losers? The African nations themselves.

African leaders are not as dumb as the Western press portrays them to be. They are not all neo-colonialist agents as Black militants think they are. They sometimes make statements or pursue certain courses of actions which you and I do not approve of, but let me again refer you to a Ghanaian proverb because I find the proverbs of my people full of great wisdom, "If you have your hands locked in the teeth of someone you do not start banging on his head." They know the extent to which their trade and economies are controlled by the Western nations. They have to move cautiously in their demands and agitation. If they did not they would be in serious economic trouble. It's a vicious circle, tightly-knit. The only thing that can break through is a strong united effort of Africans and peoples of African descent.

In their failure to get the buyers to agree on a stabilized world price for their produce, African governments turn their attention to their friends in the West for something that in everyday language one might call loans. In dignified language it is called aid. Aid comes in various forms. Most of them really are more in the interest of the donor countries than of the recipient ones. I was amazed at the number of Americans I ran into who thought that U.S. aid to Africa, for instance, was a handout which was never meant to be repaid. They do not understand that "aid" means loans, not gifts.

I answered several questions on aid in my talks, but there have been Americans, notably congressional aides, teachers and tourists who used their government's aid to African nations to embarrass some African embassies.

Under our regulations, groups of Americans visiting the embassy had to make their requests to the embassy two weeks in advance. We had found it necessary to make this regulation because, except in summer, it was impossible to cope with the number of visitors. Two weeks' notice would allow the embassy to see if some groups could be combined and also what type of program should be laid out.

Congressional aides, often just summer interns, would call the embassy and use the name of a senator or a congressman to try to get a group of students from a certain congressional district to visit the embassy within twenty-four hours. Sometimes we could oblige, but if we tried to explain it would be impossible, the aide immediately assumed the upper hand. He or she pointed out the fact that he could get his congressman to look into the possibilities of aid cuts. We were similarly threatened by some tourists who walked into the embassy and demanded a visa on three hours' notice. These people make the whole idea of aid very humiliating.

No matter how you look at it, aid becomes humiliating. To qualify for it, no African nation can truly have a neutral foreign policy of its own. It has to be prepared to go along with certain policies of the donor country even though it may disagree sharply with these policies. Every African country says boldly that its foreign policy is based strictly on neutrality and yet if you carefully examine its record you come out with the fact that it is either pro-West or pro-East. Neutrality has no meaning.

Kwame Nkrumah, probably the first African leader to make Africans aware of the term "neo-colonialism," accepted a $42,000,000 investment from Kaiser Corporation of America, even though the terms of the agreement turned out to be more beneficial to Kaiser than to Ghana. Kaiser brought jobs and became the biggest consumer of electricity from the Volta River Project. Nkrumah closed his eyes to the unfavourable terms of the agreement as he did with so many others, especially those with the East European countries.

Disillusionment with the West has often led to flirtation with the East European countries. Some African leaders are tempted to take at face value the political propaganda of the Eastern nations, notably the Soviet Union and China. Ghana was strongly influenced by their propaganda. We accepted them as sincere friends, but our experiments have proved to us that "A witch is a witch whether he is dead or living." No foreign power is interested in any developing country just for the sake of friendship. It calculates to see what benefits it will derive before it puts out aid. There is no aid that has no strings attached. It was not known until Nkrumah's overthrow, for instance, that the Ghana government never even received a blueprint of the atomic reactor that the Soviet Union was building for Ghana. And the Soviet Union was supposedly Ghana's number-one ally then.

Like the U.S., France was originally opposed to the recognition of the People's Republic of China. Of the numerous former French territories in Africa only Guinea and Mali recognized China. The rest all declined, condemning China's policy of aggression. When France reversed her decision, her former territories, one after another, declared they would follow suit.

On Monday October 25th, 1971, the Albanian resolution calling for the admission of Peoples Republic of China into the U.N. and the expulsion of Nationalist China came up before the General Assembly. In the crucial debate several African states which had traditionally voted against People's China switched allegiance. They went a degree further and voted for Formosa's expulsion.

When the results of the debate were announced, many Americans, perhaps for the first time, saw on television African jubilation. The *New York Times* later identified the jubilant Africans as the delegation from Tanzania. Official U.S. reaction to the expulsion of Taiwan and the jubilation was one of indignation. The White House itself described the Tanzanian action as "a shocking demonstration of undisguised glee." Just as many observers suspected, the U.S. unofficially threatened to cut, suspend or cease giving aid to all those small countries that had supported the Albanian resolution.

U.S. aid to developing nations suddenly became a matter of great interest and discussion. The subject followed me wherever I went—at dinner parties, at school and college engagements. In private conversations with my own friends, in shops where assistants detected my accent, I found myself being called upon to justify U.S. aid to other nations. I was happy that I did not have to do the cocktail circuit. It became evident that very few of the people I met in Washington did actually support foreign aid. The outcome of the U.N. debate on China helped to bring to the surface what the feelings of the average American were on foreign aid.

The big question is why did several African nations who have traditionally refused to recognize China's existence or who have maintained a policy of two Chinas switch positions? The U.S. State Department seemed as puzzled as the ordinary man over our action. The so-called experts on African Affairs, or the "Africa watchers" if you like, failed to see that the U.S. itself had helped the African nations to adopt a new attitude towards People's China. Since independence many of the African nations have known that their China policies were unrealistic. They refused to recognize China for two fundamental reasons: (1) U.S. is the country "from whom all blessings flow." Recognition of a country with whom the U.S. was not on speaking terms would be suicidal. (2) Genuine fear that China exports subversion into your country once you develop friendship with her.

Like a bolt out of the blue the U.S. announces one day that its President was to visit China. Incredible! (1) The U.S. does not recognize China. (2) Power and wealth breed arrogance. The U.S. is powerful and wealthy. From our point of view it does not need China. It can recognize China without its President visiting the land. (3) Mr. Kissinger had secretly visited China to make the arrangements of the visit. So the U.S. was courting China. None of this made sense.

From that day we learned that the world balance of power had changed. The U.S., on whose account we had snubbed China, was changing its policy. It was like taking sides in a quarrel between two friends. If we, the developing nations, continued to take sides we would eventually be the losers. No one ever thought that the U.S. would court China in such a dramatic way. What guarantees do we have that the U.S. and China would not one day become the greatest allies? We woke up. We acted realistically.

We have also had to pay the price of our action. Like a father chiding a son, the U.S. has in effect told Africa and all the other nations that look up to her for aid, "Look, sonny, for being naughty you're not going to get any more allowance." Some observers, including myself, saw the U.S. action as childish. Others thought it was humiliating. But whatever label we gave to it I am personally gratified by the sequence of events. It will help the African nations themselves to learn to depend more on their own human and natural resources and to reduce their financial, moral and psychological dependence on the U.S. and other nations. One great damage that colonialism and slavery has done to our people is to put them in a position of looking up to Whites. Neither colonialism or slavery treated us as equals to our bosses. The relations were that of a master and his servant. Independence and abolition of slavery have not yet totally destroyed our lack of self-confidence and that dependence on Whites. Every White man, in the eyes of the African, is rich. So any White man traveling through Africa is deluged with requests for money by children.

Now that the U.S. is gradually making it known that it does not wish to continue with its foreign aid program, the African nations should begin to hammer into the heads of their people that sacrifices are required. The people must pay for all projects.

I see dissatisfaction among the people. Some of the countries may resort undoubtedly to military coups, as did Ghana early in 1972, but military coups will not be the answer to the problem. The answer will be to educate the people to the facts. The African governments must also be prepared to reduce unnecessary and wasteful expenditure.

African nations should realize that the governments of the donor nations are made up of human beings who are as vulnerable as they are. No one likes to give aid just for the sake of giving it. It would be unrealistic for us to expect that the U.S. or any other country would give aid without trying to manipulate the receiving country. We should begin to explore areas where we can help ourselves. In some instances our people have no reason whatsoever to play second fiddle to anybody.

There may be some who will disagree sharply with me that the African nations should try to do away with foreign aid. One may be President Hubert Maga of Dahomey whose contention, if the newspapers are to be believed, is that foreign aid to Africa is only a return of a

231

small percentage of what colonialists have exploited from Africa for years, and that no one should be opposed to aid.

Hubert Maga is right, but right or wrong I look forward to the day when African nations will try to reduce their dependence on foreign aid and Black Americans reduce their dependence on welfare. That is the only time we will be able to call ourselves men and sing "Before I become your slave I'll see you in your grave."

So far, I have discussed some of the problems which have stifled economic and social growth in a large number of African nations. There are more—some that my mind, untrained in economics, cannot discuss. There is yet another that I choose to discuss rather reluctantly since it might make some people think that I blame all of Africa's economic ills on the developed nations.

What has been happening in African countries is that since independence, practically all of the African nations have continued to maintain their historic and economic links with their former colonial masters. The argument for this gravitation is that such associations are necessary for a smooth economic transition and development. But what this association has done is allow some of the powers, notably France, to manipulate the leaders of its former colonies.

Some of the African nations which were under France's rule are not economically viable. They are so small and poor that one wonders why a foreign power would colonize them to begin with and why, after independence, that foreign power would still hold on to them. Independence has brought them nothing but a series of economic troubles. If potentially rich nations like Ghana, Nigeria, Kenya, Uganda, Congo, Ivory Coast and a few more are still struggling, I cannot see how the others, as poor as they are, could survive. In the fear that they might go down, the very poor of the former French African nations, together with those that are viable, still hold on to France. The leaders are so deeply buried in the old French colonial policy that dependent states are not only colonies but a part of metropolitan France, that they cannot disengage themselves from that power.

The potentially rich countries have made a gain through continued association with France. Besides aid, France encourages its industrialists to invest in these former rich colonies. A visit to these countries reveals physical progress. On the surface, there is an economic boom. But beneath it, it is France and Frenchmen who control the economy. The Africans provide the labor. So long as the Africans have jobs they will not rise up against the government.

Naturally, this poses a problem to the poorer former colonies. There is uncertainty as to whether a closer relationship with France would yield dividends or not. In the mid-sixties Japan tried to break France's economic hold on the French-speaking African states along the West Coast. France resisted. It still maintains its trade and economic power over these nations.

Ultimately, such strong attachments stand in the way

of African economic unity and development.Some of us have had cause to suspect strongly that one reason the Organization of African Unity in Addis Ababa has been ineffective in making any concrete decisions is the betrayal of O.A.U. decisions to some of the former colonial powers.

During visits of heads of state to a country, one of the subjects that the receiving head of state asks the visitor to brief him on is the latter's recent meetings and discussions with other colleagues. Knowing of such protocol, I am shocked at the number of French-speaking African leaders who board the place for France shortly after the O.A.U. meetings are over. In France, they are received by the head of state. I believe that O.A.U. deliberations are discussed at these meetings.

What we have had so far is a sudden change of mind by the same heads of state who were a party to decisions taken in the conference room. Where they do not change their minds they drag their feet, making it impossible for a quorum to be reached.

Foreign powers have interest in economic and political developments in Africa. If the African nations agreed to unite economically, they would become a threat to some of the developed nations. Markets might be lost. So nine years since its founding the O.A.U. is still an ineffective forum. Our leaders go there to agree to disagree.

Petty jealousies among African leaders have also hindered progress. To help the African nations to help themselves, the United Nations Organization created the Economic Commission for Africa (E.C.A.) with head-quarters in Addis Ababa. It has recruited a very efficient staff. What the committee has sought to do is to assist in the creation of Regional Economic Councils and a Common Market to expand and promote inter-state trade. This would help to ease some of the economic burden on the African states by making it possible for them to plan industries, universities, and research jointly. More trade would also be promoted between the African states than has hitherto existed.

Again, our delegations meet at meetings sponsored by the E.C.A., this time on the ministerial level. They talk for hours on end. Nigeria, Liberia, Guinea and Mauritania cannot agree on the site of a joint iron and steel mill proposed by the Economic Commission. Rather than pulling their resources together to build a viable complex, each state thinks it has enough of its own material to feed its own mill.

Universal injustices against people of Black skin, coupled with my own frustration at my people's inability to provide a strong, united effort in anything, sometimes drive me to a point where I believe a story accredited to an elderly Black Rhodesian. According to him, the reason for the plight of the Black man on this earth is our own intrusion into a world in which the Creator had no room for us. God was so tired after creation that he dozed for a few minutes. It was during God's sleep that the Black man sneaked into the world because he could not understand why everything in the world was White. When God woke up and saw what had happened, He told the Black man he had no place on earth and would have to suffer for his intrusion.

But my Ambassador has a better version of the story of creation. It is this version that keeps me alive and well in spite of all odds.

Addressing a group of Black Americans in Washington, Ambassador Debrah said:

We often read the story about creation. The Jewish theologian created Adam and Eve in the garden of Eden, explaining creation according to his circumstances. Our elders also created a different story to explain creation according to our circumstances: how men came to be Black or White. The Good Lord, according to our story, created men and women, placed them in a big sack and travelled the ends of the world placing them on the continents as they became matured—the sign of maturity being evidenced by the color of the person's skin. The deep Blacks were the most mature and those of lighter skin the less mature. God first went to Africa where he set down the matured Blacks. As he travelled over Europe the impatience of those within the sacks caused the sack to tear open, releasing over the land all the light-skinned persons who were not really ready to be discharged.

Just like Cain killed his brother Abel because of

Abel's fine qualities, so the less-matured steathily enslaved his mature brother and ruled him over the centuries.

By the time my assignment in America neared its end, I was well aware that there are many different ways a society can be advanced or backward, and that technological progress is not the measure of everything.

My expectations, of course, had been too great. No country could live up to the gold-in-the-streets image America is sometimes given, so maybe some disillusionment is inevitable.

But I knew that my people should not envy another country simply for its material progress, and not consider its accompanying social and spiritual values. The uses to which a nation's wealth is put are more important than the amount of its wealth.

As I began thinking of seeing Ghana once more, I asked myself, and others, what the future might hold for my big, many-sided host country.

The answer was disturbing.

10

What Time
is It?
It is Now

If there is one situation which I try to avoid like the plague in the course of my assignment, it is informal get-togethers of young Black and White intellectuals. They begin with a telephone call: "Hey Fred. I have a few friends coming by for drinks. Nothing special. Why don't you come along?"

They arrive in blue jeans, bell-bottom pants and "Dashikis." They squat on the floor. Politics and politicians become the subject of conversion. It drifts to ecology, inflation and then the inevitable—race. A White man makes a remark. It could have been made because of mischievous intentions to insult. It could have been a perfectly innocent remark, or it could have even been made out of miscalculation.

Whatever it was a Black man is provoked. The room becomes electrified. With the two locked in argument, the other guests are mostly silent. In Ghana, other guests would pressure the two sides to forgive, forget, and stop being an embarrassment to their host. In America, some grab their coats and make for the door. Others sit quietly, throwing in a word here and there.

I was leaving the Wedgewood Room of the Sylvania Hotel in Philadelphia. My assignment for that evening was over. For three days and three nights, I had been involved in the 1970 orientation program for volunteers who were preparing to leave for Ghana with the Peace Corps. That evening I had had to discuss with the volunteers a subject that I do not like to discuss with friends, let alone strangers—sex. Originally, I had been asked to talk about patterns of cultural behavior among the Ghanaian people. Questions had been asked as to whether or not the volunteers could be friendly with members of the opposite sex while they were in Ghana. How intimate, some asked, could they be with their friends?

I was thankful when the time came for me to end the session. As I left the room, I was interrupted several times by some of the volunteers who were as shy as I am about talking publicly on sex. Each one had a question that had to be asked and answered privately. Just as I reached the lobby and was waiting for the elevator, I saw Rudi, one of the volunteers. Rudi was a very agreeable person. I had been asked by a friend in Washington to look him up.

"Fred, could we talk some more? I really enjoyed tonight's discussion."

I looked at the clock. It was eleven, and a friend was to pick me up in the early hours of the morning for Atlantic City. Still, I knew that I could not refuse Rudi that privilege.

Rudi was expecting a long distance call from his fiancee so we agreed to meet in his room for our discussion. We bought sodas from the machines. As we walked through the hallway to his room, all the doors of the rooms occupied by the volunteers were thrown wide open. This was their last night. They could no longer wait to get to Ghana. Every one of them was busy packing.

Butch and Glynn, two of the Black volunteers, were sitting on the floor of their room when we reached their door. "Hey," Glynn shouted in the unmistakable southern accent that I enjoy hearing, "You folks going to have a party?" Before I had time to say that we were heading to Rudi's room for a private discussion, his friend added "We will be right there."

I was a little unhappy about this, not so much at the prospect of another of those dismal Black and White confrontations but at the fact that our private discussion might not be private, after all.

We had barely entered the room when Butch, true to his word, walked in. In one arm was a portable record player. In another was a stack of albums. Glynn followed. Rudi's own two roommates arrived. Two other volunteers from the next room came. The little hotel room was suddenly crowded and noisy. Everyone was quaffing beer.

Until that night, I had no idea that Whites could curse and swear that much. Whites had always been restrained in their choice of certain words around me. I had partially come to accept that Blacks cursed so much simply because it was part of the Black experience. (A Ghanaian friend of mine who seemed troubled by Black cursing once remarked that he suspected that many of American Blacks were "Gas"—a Ghanaian tribe which is noted for cursing.) But that night, the ten White youths outclassed the two Blacks in the art of cursing. They had let down their hair.

The race issue crept in, but the discussants seemed tolerant of each other. "Be quiet, Whitey," one of the Blacks would yell, and "Watch it, Nigger," a White replied.

"Which ones—the White Niggers or the Black ones?" another asked.

I had been nervous all evening. Even though there was a feeling of good-humored give and take, the get-together might still end up like several others that I had been to. I do not like beer, but everyone else was drinking it. I drank two cans. They helped me to relax.

Suddenly, it happened. The irony of it was that I triggered what followed. At the peak of our discussion, I realized that sandwiched between me and one of the Black volunteers, Butch, was a timid-looking White who had not said a word all evening. He just listened, and made no contribution. He looked so sad and timid that I could not help what I asked: "Hey, man, are you comfortable with Blacks?"

"Not really." He admitted what I had already suspected.

"Why are you going to Africa then?"

"Well, they are different. Don't you think so?" he answered quietly.

The rest of the crowd was buried in a discussion so no one really heard my question and the answer it received except Butch. I knew Butch did not like it. I was afraid that he might jump on the youth verbally. Before he could start, I asked the White youth to tell me what it was about Blacks that made him uncomfortable. Butch interrupted me.

"Fred," he began, "this discussion on race just makes me sick. Since time immemorial, our people have talked about it. We're still where we were. Attitudes haven't changed. It seems to me that attitudes harden on the White side each time one of them makes a concession. I am done. Please don't ask him for his reasons. I have got my troubles. He's got his. If he wants to add to his troubles a fear of me, it is his problem."

I began to think about what Butch had said. He was no longer, it seemed to me, interested in trying to gain acceptance from the White youth, or from any other person for that matter. If a White person wanted to talk, Butch would talk on equal terms, but would never play a subservient role. He was not even interested in friendship with Whites.

242

Before this conversation, I had been frequently asked by some Whites why Blacks now insist on being called "Blacks" when a few years ago, any such reference would have been deemed discriminatory. I was asked why at a time when Whites were learning to accept "Negroes," the Negroes were rebuffing White efforts? I had never seriously considered these questions until Butch made it explicitly clear that he was at the end of his tether.

It suddenly became clear to me that within my three and a half years in the U.S. I had seen evidences of Black frustration building into Black hostility—a hostility which I personally think is justified and yet, because of my own dread of hate and violence, still worries me.

I thought of a few militant Black friends who would not sit in my apartment for a drink or a meal if I made the mistake of inviting any of my White friends. And I thought of several other incidents.

In 1969, the embassy played host to about two hundred Black students from Washington area colleges as part of our publicity effort. A film of Ghanaian music and dance was shown. One portion of the film showed American Peace Corps volunteers in Ghana learning to play Ghanaian musical instruments. The volunteers filmed all happend to be White. When that portion of the film was shown, the embassy building was literally rocking. The reaction was near-violent. The students booed and whistled. I turned to one student who stood behind me, asking "What's wrong?"

"Them White folks ain't got no business messing

around with those instruments. They ain't got no soul."

Three weeks after that incident, a group of teachers from Chicago visited the embassy. On their way out, they asked for some brochures on Ghana. I distributed the materials, but I found as I reached one Black female teacher that copies of one particular brochure were all gone. Before I could get one for her, she just turned and snatched a copy from a White colleague, with the words, "You White folks have always had it good. Here we come to our own soil and you're still having it good."

One day a Black child was lying in the middle of 16th Street. She had been hit by a car. The blood flowed as she lay there waiting for the ambulance. A White woman dashed to the child and started to wife off the blood with her handkerchief. The crowd of Black spectators shouted at her to leave the child alone.

At the Atlanta Congress of African Peoples, one trio brought a White drummer. As soon as he walked on the stage the crowd almost brought the Moorehouse University gymnasium down with shouts of "No, No, No, No, No, No." The trio gave in.

I could never persuade my young friends to read the book "Soul Sister," in which a White woman, through medication, changed the color of her skin to Black to experience what it was like to live Black in the U.S. They insisted that the author was not telling them anything they did not know. The only thing they could think was that she was being patronizing. I disagreed.

I knew of friends who objected strongly to their

mothers being glued to the television each Thursday night to hear the "Blue-eyed soul brother, Tom Jones." Jones had a great appeal for middle-aged women, but my friends thought Blacks could do without Jones' imitation of Black artists.

These experiences and observations, I ultimately discovered, had not sufficiently prepared me for my strange meeting with Calvin, a Black college student working at a luxurious hotel in Florida to make money to pay for his college education, and the frightful, blood-chilling conversation which ensued. Under normal circumstances, I would not have dreamed of staying in a hotel that expensive. I had done it for a foolish but emotional reason.

I lay on the beautiful, lush green lawn around the pool of the hotel trying very hard to forget the problem that had driven me to take refuge there. As much as I tried, my thoughts were still fully occupied with it. I sighed and rolled over on the lawn. Our eyes—mine and the young Black man in white uniform—met. In his hands were the silver tray and my Manhattan. "Your drink, Sir."

"Thank you. How much is it?" I asked.

"Dollar-fifty, Sir."

That formality was becoming irksome. The use of "Sir" by American salesmen, store assistants, desk officers and others irritated me. I knew they did not mean it. They used it as a matter of course.

""Please cut out that business of 'Sir," I said impatiently. "I can't stand it."

"The Management insists on it, *Sir,*" he replied.

"I don't need it. You're about my age and my color," I told him.

"You wouldn't be here if you were ...."

I looked at him again. For the first time he could not control a devilish smile.

"I've got to be going back to work, Sir," he said and started to leave.

"Hey, wait a minute," I shouted. "What's your name? Mine is Fred. Fred Hayford."

"I am Calvin, Mr. Hayford. Calvin Merriman."

"Hey, listen, Calvin. Is there any place here that Black folks hang around for entertainment?"

"You mean you want to go down as low as that—be with us?" But this time I could see he was joking.

At ten o'clock that night, Calvin and I were on the road. We travelled a few miles away in his car to a neighborhood that turned out to be Black and poor.

A sense of belonging seized me when Calvin and I entered the bar: the Black faces, the flashy clothes, the rhythmic movements of bodies—the expression which Black African men wear when they see a woman they desire, the frivolous chatter of the Black African woman when she wants to attract male attention.

As we made our way through the dancers, completely mesmerized by James Brown's "I Feel All Right," a young woman grabbed me by the hand: "Hey, Mister, I dig you. Come on, let's dance." Before I could oblige, she was snapping her fingers, moving her body and singing—

"Hey, Hey, I feel all right; mm, mm!" The place was a beautiful experience. It was a meeting of the souls and bodies of Black people. I felt at home.

After that dance, Calvin, who had taken a table in a secluded corner of the club, beckoned to me to join him. Wiping the sweat from my face, I said, "You know, Cal, it's my mother's theory that God fairly distributes his gifts. She says there is no one human being who has more than the others, either by way of material things or problems. It just so happens that we are all so busy grabbing and envying everybody else that we tend to pity ourselves. Maybe the Black man isn't so displaced, after all."

Calvin looked at me thoughtfully. "What made you say that?"

"Look at all these people. They're happy. In spite of all of the Black man's trouble, we're the same wherever you find us. We relax. We enjoy ourselves. That's probably the only way we manage to survive," I told him.

He shook his head sadly. "Black folks—they are all the same. Give them music, food, liquor and something in skirts, and they forget. But you know Fred, I disagree with your mother. Tell me one thing we Blacks have that we can honestly feel God has fairly given us. We've got no power, no money and no influence. And the Bible says 'them that got shall have!' The only way we can change that is through a revolution."

"A revolution?" I stared at my new friend in disbelief.

"Fred, I don't know what kind of a revolution, but there is one thing I can assure you. When the time comes, no Black man is going to say to another, 'People get ready for the train to Jordan'."

"Fred, if ever you have a chance to fly over the Mississippi River, look at it. Look at it, man. What you see is not mud, it is the blood of my ancestors. Their bodies have been dumped so often into that river it's not funny. Fred, I am from Alabama and I know what I am talking about." Tears welled in his eyes.

"I know this can't go on forever, Calvin, but talk about a bloody revolution sounds hideous to me. Mind you, it's our people I'm worried about. In the event of any Black uprising our people will be wiped off this earth in one minute. If the U.S. is using the weapons at its disposal against its own young people, Cal, believe me it won't hesitate to use them against us. And please don't talk to me about world opinion helping us because world opinion is White."

"What has the Black man here got to live for, anyway? When you have gone through our experience maybe death is the only time your soul begins to experience freedom."

"Do you see young Whites playing any role in a revolution of that kind?" I asked him, fascinated by the depth of his feelings.

"None," Calvin snapped.

I had asked that question because of the adoption of Black Panther slogans by various young White organizations—militant and non-militant. I had also been amazed by the number of White youths who were shaping their hair into "Afros." I had feared that in the event of an uprising young Whites would join hands with Blacks, but Cal quickly dismissed this.

"Calvin, don't you think the White man really needs us?"

"He sure does. He can't afford to do away with us. He needs our strength. Our resources and our support. We're an economic backbone for him. Our purchasing power alone is thirty billion dollars a year. Thirty billion, Fred. I know that the White man needs you, too, and by that I mean Africa. A classic study is Nigeria. See how unhappy both the U.S. and Britain were over Russia's role in the Nigerian conflict. Just read our papers. The West sees Communists hiding behind every tree in Africa. And the Communists see Imperialists behind every tree in Africa. All the world powers have their eyes on Africa, because they need you. If your politicians were playing their cards well, they could get the best out of both worlds without giving anything in return," Calvin said.

Later he added, "You see, unless this country is destroyed and built again, attitudes would be the same. Our children will collect the ashes together and rebuild what we have destroyed; but what we destroy in disunity they will build in unity. In other words, America needs to be born again." He believed it implicitly.

Suddenly I realized that I was no longer listening to Calvin. The conversation had been for me deep and a little frightening. My mind wondered into the unknown future. All I saw was bleakness and hopelessness. Just then the words of one of my favorite blues came rushing into my mind. To break the silence that had come between us and also to brighten things up a little, I wanted to sing that particular blues, but remembering that I had no voice at all but something that sounds like a broken record, elected to say the words out loud:

> Trouble in mind
> I am blue,
> But I won't be blue always.
> The sun is gonna shine
> In my back door someday.

I called the airlines two days later and asked for my flight to Washington to be changed. I no longer wanted a direct flight. I wanted to fly over the Mississippi River. As luck would have it the pilot on the flight not only informed us when we were hovering over the Mississippi but flew at a height that made it possible for me to take a good look at it. As I looked I recollected every word Calvin had uttered. Fear gripped me. I wondered how many Calvin Merrimans America has bred and continues to breed. If there were many, I said, then there had better be a change of heart and attitudes; people should begin to look at people as people—or may the Almighty God have mercy on all our souls.

Index